Advance Praises for *The 'Other' Shangri-La*

Even though China has been open to foreign tourists for more than 40 years, few make it to the magical, mountainous border region between Sichuan and Tibet that inspired the legend of 'Shangri-La'. But in this engaging and profound work, Shivaji Das takes us there, helping us to understand the fraught relations between Han Chinese and minority groups, and the country's vibrant religious scene. Mostly, *The 'Other' Shangri-La* is an ode to this beautiful alpine region and its people, with the author's empathy and humanity making him a most excellent companion.

—**Ian Johnson**
Pulitzer Prize-winning author of *The Souls of China: The Return of Religion After Mao*

Shivaji discovers meaningful moments in his travels, and evokes the environment and history of the place in his writing, connecting the present and the past. Indeed, for a deeper understanding of ourselves, we need to weave our lives closely with everything that surround us.

—**Ma Jian**
Author of *Red Dust: The Noodle Maker, Stick Out Your Tongue, Beijing Coma, The Dark Road, China Dream*

Shivaji and Lobo bring alive the unchartered territories of China in a way that you travel along with them. They bring out the life in the obscure hills in a way that you feel like a co-traveller with them, alternating between tourist jaunts and pristine landscapes, between human habitation and solitude.
—Anuradha Goyal
Author and Top Travel Blogger

Buckle up – you're in for the trip of a lifetime! The intrepid Shivaji Das takes the reader–and his good-natured wife Lobo–along the Sichuan-Tibet Highway, 'one of the most dangerous roads in the world', stopping on the way to spend the night with nomads (and their yaks); ascend to the world's highest town, and go down to the valley of beauties, among other adventures. This informative travelogue is often funny, and sometimes scary, but always entertaining.
—Suzanne Kamata
Author of *Squeaky Wheels: Travels with My Daughter by Train, Plane, Tuk-tuk, Metro and Wheelchair*

In equal measures informative and witty, Shivaji Das takes his readers along the dangerous roads of Sichuan's Tibetan regions where monasteries and mountains meet with neon lights and rapid development. Never romanticizing, *The 'Other' Shangri-La* captures the region's cultural complexities while affirming travel's capacity to transform.
—Piia Mustamaki
Essayist, Travel Writer and Lecturer of Writing at New York University, Abu Dhabi

The 'Other' Shangri-La

Journeys through the Sino-Tibetan frontier in Sichuan

Shivaji Das

KONARK

Konark Publishers Pvt Ltd
New Delhi • Seattle

Konark Publishers Pvt Ltd
206, First Floor,
Peacock Lane, Shahpur Jat,
New Delhi - 110 049
Tel : +91-11-4105 5065
Mob : +91-93552 93900, +91-93552 94900
e-mail : india@konarkpublishers.com
website : www.konarkpublishers.com

Konark Publishers International
8615, 13th Ave SW,
Seattle, WA 98106
Phone : (415) 409-9988
e-mail : us@konarkpublishers.com

Cataloging in Publication Data--DK
  Courtesy: D.K. Agencies (P) Ltd. <docinfo@dkagencies.com>

    Das, Shivaji, author.
The 'other' Shangri-La : journeys through the Sino-Tibetan frontier in Sichuan / Shivaji Das.
    pages cm
    Includes bibliographical references.
    ISBN 9788194201861
1. Das, Shivaji--Travel--China--Tibet Autonomous Region.
2. Tibet Autonomous Region (China)--Description and travel.
3. Tibet Autonomous Region (China)--Social life and customs--21st century.   I. Title.

LCC DS786.D37 2020 | DDC 915.1505   23

Editor: Dipali Singh
Cover jacket: Misha Oberoi
Cover image: Shivaji Das
Printed and bound at Thomson Press (India) Ltd

The Song of the Khampa man

Oh...
The Khampa man in my heart
His forehead fully written with
Ancestors' stories
The clouds carry their laughter, carry their laughter
The chest is ambition
And the grassland of love
Let the women hate me
Flying freely
In the veins
Echoing sound of horse hoofs
In my eyes is the holy sun
Wine in my heart
Singing
The world is in my hand, in my hand...

Contents

The Journey Route

Prologue

This was Tibet but yet, not Tibet. This was frontier land—the western half of Sichuan where the plains mingled with the mighty Qinghai-Tibetan plateau and the cultures of the Tibetans and Hans, the majority ethnic group of China, overlapped. Dotted with magical vistas, this was also the land where the Sino-Tibetan conflict, even though sporadic, was at its most intense. Qualifiers, such as Sino, Tibetan and Chinese, can cause immense debate and since political, historical and geographical correctness are nearly impossible to achieve in this situation, I have used these qualifiers rather loosely throughout this book. I have also altered the real names of most of the people we met along our journey. This book is a travelogue and should not be seen as an attempt to provide any verdict on the conflict.

Finally, this book would not have been possible without Yolanda Yu (fondly known as Lobo))—my wife and travel partner—who translated whatever the locals said and whatever I wanted to ask and most importantly, again proved to be the person I would plead to come along for any trip to anywhere.

One

Again, and Once Again

Nasty bump number 329. The bus skidded, throwing me off my seat to allow me that split-second look at the angry river of death flowing a thousand feet below. The driver, despite being always on the phone, managed to make a Super Racer turn—a Grand Escape. I thanked the white letters engraved on the rock facing us, the Tibetan mantra *Om Mani Padme Hum*. I thanked the red letters carved on the rock next to it: 'Long Live the Communist Party.' The views of the snow-capped mountains all around us brought back the calm in me.

We were travelling along the 2,142-km-long Sichuan–Tibet Highway or Highway 318, one of the most dangerous roads in the world. Truck drivers did not consider fellow mates as men unless they had dared and survived Highway 318.

Lobo was still clutching my fist with the strength of Rambo. The monk sitting across the aisle was throwing up. One passenger yelled, 'That's it. You son of a bitch of a driver! You have had enough fun. Get me down right now!' He ambled through the aisle gingerly, continuing the barrage of expletives. Once he got down at a stop, a no-man's land, we all stuck out our faces from the windows, just to make sure that he was not taking away our luggage.

Peace followed and our van continued galloping over the unpaved road. The driver got back to his phone. Below, the mad river flowed on and on. Occasionally, from the other direction, a van rushed at us. Rhythmically, the passengers cleared their throats and spat in the plastic bags tactfully placed next to each seat. A little later, the bus stopped for a toilet break. The guardian of the toilet, an unimpressed elderly Tibetan lady, thrust a wad of one-yuan notes with their Chairman Mao faces at us. Inside, men sat evenly spaced with their heads down and bums bared. I remember looking down at a thousand plastic bottles and cups that once contained instant noodles. I wondered why the cups were there. Were they eaten up as well?

Once we boarded the bus again, the driver turned on the television to unleash Tibetan music videos upon us—each song's beat sounding exactly the same as the one before and each video resembling the earlier one with blue skies, green fields, snow mountains, young Tibetans dancing in circles with arms wide open, and the lead singer modulating his voice as if he was being spanked hard. The road became even more miserable. The driver seemed nervous for the first time. He turned off the music. The Tibetan women sitting next to us chanted mantras in anxious voices, blowing and bursting chewing gum at the same time. A young monk sitting behind us began vomiting. To comfort him, his neighbour began playing *Om Mani Padme Hum* on his phone. Hadn't I heard this song before—in a spa in Singapore?

Two

The Planning

We had planned this trip after drooling over postcards—of the gorgeous mountain landscapes—picked up at a travel agent's office in China. The trip promised hardship—cold hotels, life-threatening drives and 30 days of living above 12,000 feet. A conversation with a friend, who had been on this journey a few years back, ignited my biggest fear of travelling to China's hinterland.

'There are no toilets in hotels,' she said. 'You have to use communal toilets. And you know how they are in China.'

Hearing this, I began to shiver.

'Can't we visit this place after a decade, instead of

now?' I asked Lobo.

For most of my conscious life, I have been woken up halfway through my sleep by one recurrent dream of me stepping into one detestable toilet. Lobo knew this. So she gave a barrage of assurances, churning out China's latest economic data and the successes of its space programme. She searched for pictures of toilets on Weibo, the most popular microblogging site in China.

'Look,' she said, 'If things were really that bad, this search-word about dirty toilets would have been blocked in China.'

We booked the tickets to visit Sichuan.

We planned to start our journey from Chengdu, the capital of Sichuan province in southwest China, in October 2016. From there, we would go to Kangding, a town famous in China because of the 'Kangding Love Song', located at the edge of the Qinghai–Tibetan plateau, the roof of the world. Next, we would arrive in Tagong to stay with the Tibetan nomads, following which we would reach Litang, the Wild West of Tibetan culture, nowadays being marketed as 'The World's Highest Town'.

From Litang, we would move south to Daocheng, the gateway to the Yading Nature Reserve, a 'Five-Star Attraction' as the Chinese label their tourist destinations, also named by the local government as Shangri-La.

From Yading, we would travel north, passing by

Chengdu again to visit Sertar and Larung, a giant monastery complex that also held the dubious claim of being the largest illegal settlement in the world. We planned to end our trip at Danba, a valley famed for its beautiful women and tall medieval towers, to watch out for beauties and enemies alike.

Three

Cleaning the Ears and Clearing the Mind in Chengdu

The flight from Singapore to Chengdu was uneventful, except for one incident. When we passed by one of the gates at the Changi airport we saw an amusing sight—a group of Indonesian middle-aged ladies who appeared to be covered in snow. As we got closer, we realized that they had been barred by the security officers from carrying dozens of body lotions they had bought. In a desperate attempt, they were applying dollops of cream on themselves till each bottle carried liquid just within the permitted limit!

At Chengdu, we put up at a homestay. The owner cautioned us, saying, 'The entrance door to the apartment complex closes at 11 in the night. If you want to enter after that, you have to knock and the doorman will come. You pay him 2 yuan. Then he will open the door.'

A unique Chinese solution!

I always enjoy the first day of a trip—settling into another rhythm, another life, missing my toothbrush at its familiar place. Our window overlooked the People's Park, which was bordered by one of the busiest thoroughfares in Chengdu. As Lobo caught up on her sleep, I spent the first morning just watching this street. An old couple was crossing the street and when the man attempted to hold the lady's hand, she angrily snatched it away. A sharp-suited man was walking with a large broom he had just bought. Children hopped around in padded clothing. Migrant men from Xinjiang, obvious from their appearance, lazily manoeuvred their carts loaded with memories from their arid land, colourful small mounds of dried fruits.

That day, we decided to relax since our high-altitude hardship was soon to follow. After lunch, we visited the People's Park. We saw groups of elderly couples singing and dancing as has been an age-old custom. Recent times have not taken kindly to this wonderful tradition and complaints against loud music in such geriatric activities have forced authorities to impose severe restrictions. At Chengdu, 65 decibels was the maximum sound limit and giant decibel meters were scattered across the park to make sure people did not cross it. I couldn't help but pity the dancers, who instead of looking lovingly at their partners, kept blinking at the decibel meters.

Inside the massive park, there was a small lake where one could rent tiny boats in pastel colours. The walkway overlooking the boat-rental station had been rather elegantly named as the 'Pavilion for Watching Boats'. As we strolled, I also, of all things, spotted a Diarrhoea Clinic inside the park.

We visited a tea-house, a famed Chengdu institution where patrons could leisurely spend a whole day with a cup of decent tea for 15 to 20 yuan. As expected, half the floor in the tea-house had been covered in spit, spitting being a great Chinese pastime. Ear-cleaners in traditional uniforms moved around clinking their tongs, displaying an array of fine-pointed equipment held like chopsticks between their fingers. To give Lobo a nice photo-op, I engaged Mr Chin. Why not have clean ears before an adventure?

Mr Chin congratulated me on my decision, 'You are a smart man. You are going for a long adventure to a tough area. Cleaning your ears helps clear up your mind before that.'

Pleased with the advice, I enquired more about Mr Chin's career.

'I have been doing this for over 20 years,' Mr Chin said. 'At this same tea-house! We are like shareholders here because if we don't work here, no one will come to this tea-house.'

He charged 20 yuan for ear-cleaning while offering top-up services.

'On a bad day, I get five customers. On my best day, I get 10.'

He convinced Lobo too to add up to his numbers for the day. As he started cleaning her ears, he said, 'Girls rarely ask for our service because they are too shy to be seen in public like this. But you are a good person.'

As Mr Chin departed, he said, 'The strangest thing I have picked from someone's ears is a silkworm.'

My submission to the ear-cleaner's sales pitch made Lobo get more experimental. Before I could realise it, my hand was in the hands of a palmist she had just nodded to. These palmists, like the ear-cleaners, are also an essential feature in tea-houses.

The frail old lady said, 'You have only yourself to rely on to succeed in your life. But at the same time, no bad person will ever harm you. One characteristic of yours is that you are too soft-hearted.'

She offered to read Lobo's palms but when Lobo refused, she read her forehead instead and gave her prognosis for free, 'Be kind to other women. And as for your career, you can never expect any help from your husband, this man.'

I had expected more dramatic predictions, the typical 'everything is great, but …' She didn't push to sell any solutions either for my soft-heartedness or for my incapacity to further Lobo's career. Perhaps, she was the reincarnation of John Lennon or maybe the old lady was not really a trained palmist, just another of those migrants from the countryside trying to make a living in urban China.

Soon, I was hungry and what better place to find vegetarian food than at the Manjushri temple, one of the oldest in Chengdu, also famed for its vegetarian buffet? The approach to the temple was lined with beggars, the disabled and the mentally unsound, hoping for alms, some shouting out their grievances and blessings to patrons over loudspeakers. Ignoring their pleas, I went straight for the vegetarian buffet where a notice said that there was a 5-yuan refund if no food was wasted. That set my mind into a frenzy. How would I retrieve that 5 yuan? Instead of enjoying the food for which I had already spent 35 yuan, I conjured scheme after scheme to make my plate as well as Lobo's look clean. Eventually, I played a trick, cleaning up our plates in the trash bin just when no one was looking. Tense, I walked up to the nun manning the cash counter, and once I got the 10 yuan back, I achieved *nirvana*.

Enlightened, I walked inside the temple to check if there was anything left to see. A signing-up booth for monks caught my attention. I looked through the register and noted that 10 people had already signed up for the initiation ceremony for the next day. A young woman asked the two elderly ladies at the counter, 'If I sign up, will I never be able to marry?'

'No problem at all,' came the response in unison from the two ever-smiling ladies, 'You can choose to be one of those monks who stay within the family.'

Our nun-wannabe was still not convinced, 'Will this show in my documents?'

'Not at all,' the duo replied in unison, 'In China, every individual has the full freedom to practise religion.'

Just before she was about to put pen to paper, another question sprang up in her mind, 'Hold on,' she looked alarmed. 'Will I have to pay?'

'Not at all,' came the synchronized reply, 'Not only is it free, we will also give you a mantra book and a rosary for free.'

At that very moment, another name got added to the queue for a Buddhist heaven.

To make a soft landing into Tibetan culture, we spent the evening at Chengdu's Tibetan quarters. Chengdu is the largest Tibetan city outside of the Qinghai–Tibetan plateau with more than 30,000 resident Tibetans and a floating Tibetan population of 150,000 to 200,000.[1] The streets of 'Little Lhasa' had its fair share of 'Chinese Dream' posters. On both sides of this 'Parkour Street' were shops selling all things Tibetans need—incense sticks, prayer flags, thankha posters, monk robes and handheld prayer wheels. There were beads, beads and more beads hung up densely from the shop walls, spread out in heaps on the pavement by upstart sellers, attracting robed monks looking for a prayer counter and teenage girls looking for a cheap fashion fix. Some shops were galleries of bodhisattva statues. They came in all sizes—from palmtops to giants suitable for the most ambitious temple halls—all gilded, their eyes casting that piercing glance of Tibetan Buddhism.

As we walked along the Tibetan quarter, we spotted a nomad getting a haircut, with his locks covering the entire floor. A middle-aged Tibetan couple was sitting on the curbstones by the road, looking lovingly at each other although the man kept counting prayer beads all the while. At a Tibetan bookshop, the entrance was lined up with books on Xi Jinping, President of the People's Republic of China, and government brochures on how to obtain a passport, arguably a difficult endeavour for any Tibetan. The police presence in this area was heavy. With so many Tibetans around, the authorities perhaps feared that anything could happen anytime. But to keep calm, people set up impromptu stalls on the streets as soon as the sun set, selling yogurt made of yak milk.

I prepared myself in another way for the trip, by getting my hair shaved off at a Chengdu salon. I attracted quite a crowd at the salon as the staff and some passers-by surrounded me to witness what surprises my scalp would reveal once it was denuded of hair. When nothing worthy of gossip appeared, I tried to compensate for their time by entertaining them with my wisdom.

'I do two things every time I go for long trips,' I said to the audience through Lobo, my translator. 'Number one, I always shave off my hair and number two, I do not shave my face for the entire trip.'

'Why so?' asked the young hairdresser. 'Shouldn't you grow your hair long instead? It will be very cold where you are going.'

'That doesn't matter,' I said. 'It's simple Yin and Yang. Shave the scalp, grow the beard.'

The cashier intervened, 'It must be some kind of lucky charm for him.'

'No,' I objected. 'It is a matter of principles. And what is a man without principles?'

'We don't understand,' said the people in the crowd as they dispersed, looking puzzled.

For dinner, we met Lobo's friend and her partner at the Gesar Kitchen, an apt choice since we were soon going to tread where the legendary King Gesar once had. The king of the ancient Tibetan Ling kingdom, Gesar is the hero of the epic named after him, the greatest work of Tibetan literature, probably composed in A.D. 200. Lobo's friends, a rather congenial couple, warned us about what to avoid during our trip.

They cautioned, 'Don't drink water from any of the streams—they contain a parasite that grows within the body and there is no cure for the condition it causes; don't ask the price of any item unless you really want to buy it. You can negotiate and bargain, but walking out after asking about the price is considered very rude; beware of Tibetan dogs. Always carry some stones in your pockets and a stick. These dogs can chase you for up to 3 km, so always maintain a stock of 3 kg of stones. Stock up at Kangding, as you can get the right sizes there.'

Four

Kangding: On the Edge of Two Cultures

Our first stop on the Qinghai–Tibetan Plateau was the town of Kangding (or Dartsendo, as it is known in Tibetan). A small town of around 100,000 inhabitants, Kangding is famous for two reasons: an important stopover on the Tea Horse Trail, the commercial thoroughfare where Chinese tea and Tibetan horses were once traded, and for its love song.

The road from Chengdu to Kangding was marked by traffic jams that were actually beautiful. A journey, touted to be six hours long, yawned repeatedly and stretched itself to 10. Yet, it was made bearable by the sight of an illuminated necklace of mythical proportions, its beads made of bright car lights, red and yellow. All along this road, a string of road construction equipment scraped the earth like obsessive-compulsive monsters. They hummed, loud and clear, China's promise to Tibet for better or worse days, depending on which camp you belonged to.

As soon as we arrived at Kangding, everybody wanted us to take off for different places.

'Come with me to Mugecuo, very nice photographs you can take of the scenery, especially the lakes,' said one giant man.

'No, take my car to Tagong, nothing in Mugecuo, but beautiful grasslands and the Lhakhang Monastery in Tagong,' said another.

'Back to Chengdu tomorrow? Come with me. Nothing to see here or where they want to take you,' said a scrawny man.

This made everyone burst into laughter.

One of them asked me where I was from. Upon hearing that my nationality was Indian, they folded their hands, saying, 'We love India. That's where our Dalai Lama is.'

I was unsure how to react. Being a self-proclaimed atheist, feminist and anti-feudalist, I had mixed opinions about this man who was somehow responsible for the instant respect I was drawing here. This instant reverence for the country of my birth also made me feel as if I was one of those Buddhist luminaries who had travelled across ages from India to Tibet.

During the middle ages, it had been a matter of prestige for the various Tibetan kings and nobles to invite and sponsor masters of Buddhism from India to their provinces. The monks would then spread new teachings and new scriptures for translation and receive fabulous treatment from their Tibetan hosts. A few Indian masters, however, would be left stranded when they lost their interpreters. Since no one could understand them, these unfortunate luminaries would then be forced to live a nomadic life in a foreign land.

Unlike the masters of the days past, I had neither any messages nor any scriptures. But I had Lobo, a more trustworthy interpreter. However, Lobo, who is half Han and half Manchu (Hans and Manchus are ethnic groups in China), spoke no Tibetan but for one word which she used excessively—Tashi delek or 'Greetings'. But in the sensitive political climate of Tibet, even Tashi delek had become controversial. Tibetans in China used it primarily as a greeting for Losar or the Tibetan New Year while Tibetans outside had been using it as a general greeting, both parties accusing each other of a mistake.

It was 10 p.m. and we needed to quickly find a place to sleep. At an elevation of nearly 2,600 metre, the night was getting very cold very fast. Getting a hotel was not too difficult. Anyone who saw us shouted at us to get our attention and then made the universal gesture for sleep. The room rate cards in Kangding were from another city, each asking for more than 300 yuan but the receptionists inside asked for half of what was on display. We chose the one with the most enchanting front office, a roadside fire surrounded by a group of Han ladies. One of them showed us a gallery of bedrooms and toilets on her phone screen, but we realised that it was her apartment posing as a guesthouse, showing the Han entrepreneurial spirit at its best.

It was obvious only the next morning that we had crossed into another realm. Daylight revealed bodhisattvas painted on the mountain faces, the Tibetan script on shopfront signs, and a market dripping with blood from an enormous collection of severed yak heads.

We were finally in the land of the Khams, one of the three main Tibetan groups, known for their ruggedness, ferocity, banditry and independent streak. In a culture famously obsessed with the use of honorific titles, the language of the Khams never bothered to have any such niceties. Even their monks occasionally took to robbing. The Khams are also believed to be the ancestors of the Sherpas, the famed mountaineers of Nepal.

The rugged geography of the region, comprising massive peaks and deep gorges, resulted in scattered populations whose history was largely unknown to record-keepers. But what everyone would vouch for was that the Khams would succumb to no one. They fought whoever came their way—the Central Tibetans of Lhasa, the Mongols of Karakorum and the Hans of Beijing, Nanjing and Chang'an. When the Chinese Communist Party took control, the Khams, who were averse to the Lhasa regime in Tibet, welcomed its government initially. But once their traditional structures of landownership and monastic control were being dismantled, the Khams were the first to revolt. Even today, the Khams (together with the Amdos) are the most restive in Tibetan-inhabited areas with a relatively high incidence of self-immolations in protests against Chinese rule. From time to time, therefore, the Chinese government blocked foreigners from travelling to the very areas that we planned to visit.

In a country not short of cities of monstrous proportions, Kangding seemed tiny and humble, walkable from one end to the other. Yet, at one point in history, it was a centre of political intrigue, being the capital of the Chakla kingdom squeezed in between the Mongol-Tibetan and the Chinese empires. In the mid-seventeenth century, the Dalai Lama's forces from Central Tibet forced the Chakla king to accept Lhasa's authority. But the king revolted in 1666, with support from the Qing ruler. Lhasa sent troops to take back control and, tired of the Chakla king's machinations, finally got rid of him in 1699. This provoked Qing China to act directly and the ruler responded by killing the Dalai Lama's commissioner in Kangding. Since then, the character of the town has been shifting from Tibetan to Han, as the ethnic group now constitutes a significant majority of Kangding's population. Yet, like all places born out of trade, the town still remains a relaxed melting pot of Han,

Tibetan, Yi and Hui people.

We visited a Hui restaurant for breakfast. Lobo was fascinated by the clouds of smoke rising out of the giant soup vat that fleetingly masked and revealed the youthful attendant who was spinning long strands of noodles. 'This is the most comforting sight in the world,' she said, 'It reminds me of my childhood.'

As we waited for food, the young man told us, 'We Huis are Muslim people. So, we don't serve pork here. There are many Huis in Kham. They are traders and in the olden days, traded tea between the Hans and the Tibetans. Today, they trade in caterpillar mushrooms. But my family came here only two years ago. We came from Gansu in northwest China to take over this restaurant from another Hui who had run it for 10 years.'

It was easy to fall in love with Kangding, a town trapped between hills powdered with snow and two loud rivers—the Yala and Zheduo—that galloped through its centre. Rightfully then, the town had become famous all over China because of the Kangding Love Song. Commemorating a horse ride taken by two lovers high in the mountains, the song had become a national hit in the 1950s and was still strong in the nation's memory. These days, the song was omnipresent in all karaoke playlists in China and is a key reason for domestic tourists to visit Kangding. At the town square, it was played on loudspeakers over and over again. A giant concrete block constructed to look like an open book displays the lyrics both in Mandarin and English:

"Over the (liuliu)[2] Paoma mountain, there is a
(liuliu) pure white cloud
The cloud is crowning (liuliu) Kangding (liuliu)
the town uprightly
A crescent moon, Kangding (liuliu) town...
The (liuliu) eldest sister born from Li's is (liuliu)
very pretty
The (liuliu) eldest brother born from Zhang's has
fallen in love with (liuliu) her
A crescent moon, has fallen in love with (liuliu)
her...
Firstly, his falling in love with the (liuliu) girl for
her beauty
Secondly, his falling in love with the (liuliu) girl
for her (liuliu) housework
A crescent moon, for her (liuliu) housework...
All the (liuliu) girls over the world, as much as
(liuliu) I love
All the (liuliu) boys over the world, as much as you
(liuliu) woo
A crescent moon, as much as you (liuliu) woo ..."

The Paoma mountain mentioned in the song was right in front of us and even though it was tempting, in the spirit of the song, to ride a horse over it with Lobo, we ditched the plan because we had read ominous paragraphs about it in guidebooks, threatening possible muggings along the course. As the next best thing, we just read together the lyrics of the song on the concrete tablet.

The town of love was naturally the town of babies. Soon I realised that nowhere else in China—a country of exceptionally low fertility rates—had I seen such a proliferation of babies. The mountain weather gave these babies bulging red cheeks, just like the oversized red radishes on display in the roadside stalls in Kangding.

From the town square, we walked along the river where a small gallery had been set up in memory of the porters who carried tea bricks (compressed tea) along the Tea Horse Trail, delivering tea from Yunnan and Sichuan to Tibet and further on to India, and in return, providing sturdy Tibetan horses for military use in China. The trade along this route ebbed and flowed throughout its long history, beginning from the Song dynasty period in the tenth century till the mid-twentieth century when the construction of the Sichuan–Tibet highway finally put a halt to the antlike march of humans with refrigerator-sized loads of tea bricks attached to their backs.

Though less glamorized than the Silk Road, the Tea Horse Trail was far more treacherous. Porters, mostly Han Chinese, traversed through passes over 17,000 feet high, often so narrow as to only allow one foot at a time, carrying loads of 60 to 150 kg. The trail became a graveyard for countless untimely deaths, of those who slipped or just gave in to exposure. Even today, their curse lingers on, as the Highway 318 keeps granting death, as evident from the hundreds of rusting trucks and vans that litter this unfortunate trail. But in that small stretch in Kangding, the trail had been converted into a pleasant walkway for tourists. Elderly Tibetan women stopped by to admire the flowers growing alongside. On a shaded sitting area, a Tibetan man was sketching a watch with a ballpoint pen on to his son's wrists. When we asked the boy what the time was, he blushed and ran away. Our laughter blended with the faint chanting of the monks from the nearby monastery.

We visited the Catholic church on the other side of the road. The Kham region triggered great fervour among both Catholics and Protestants because for both groups, it was the final frontier for spreading Christianity. The Catholics came first, in the mid-nineteenth century when they established a mission in Batang. The Protestants followed, landing at the turn of the twentieth century. The Khams, in keeping with their reputation, welcomed them with fire and arms, destroying the Catholic church twice, killing the priests, diehard converts, and even the Chinese officer who gave free land to the French Catholics in 1905 in a geopolitical ploy to counterbalance the ever-present threat of British occupation of Tibet. But the missions persevered and today, they boast of over 200 Catholics in Kangding and a few more in places such as Batang and Moxi.[3]

At the church, after much knocking on the door and calling out, we found an old man with a chubby face.

'I am the guard here. We usually see a lot of activity here. But people come only on Sundays,' he explained apologetically.

We had time to kill and he had tales to tell. It was obvious that he hadn't talked to people for ages.

'Sit for a while. I will tell you more.'

'The church used to hold 2,000 people once, but now there is a new church in the new town. So even on Sundays, we get only about 10 people.'

His breath reeked of alcohol and I knew his stated facts would not cut ice with researchers. But, we were not on a fact-finding mission anyway.

'I was a car mechanic for 30 years. Then I became a guard here. I am a new convert, became a Catholic only a year ago when my wife convinced me. She and her family are all Christians. And no, we don't face any discrimination because of our religion here.'

He showed us pictures from the past. 'We used to have a Swiss priest, Mr Mike Torney. Many foreigners visit this place. Just last year, there was a group of foreigner priests who came here, but I didn't understand a word they said.'

We asked him if the Pope or anyone from the Vatican had come here, braving China's rocky relationship with the Holy See.

He looked confused, 'What is Pope? Vatican? Wait, I know what you're talking about, the big church. That is located just north of Kangding. Yes, many people come from there.'

He wanted to take us to the top of the building. In his drunken state, he struggled to put the ladder against the wall.

'It's nice upstairs. We can talk more.' He looked at me, saying, 'You go first.'

The ladder had a rather tentative hold. I had a sudden fear that he would remove the ladder after I went up, so somehow, I managed to decline the offer. He looked disappointed and I felt sorry for breaking the heart of this man guarding a small church in a small town with a small history.

We visited the large monastery in Kangding where monks were too busy with prayers to engage with us. We went back to the town and came across the spring of Kangding, where a marble statue of Princess Wencheng had been erected. An adopted child of the Tang royalty, Wencheng was married off as a peace offering to Songtsen Gyampo, the founder of the Tibetan empire and the first among the three Dharma kings in the Tibetan pantheon. She, together with Princess Bhrikuti of Nepal, another wife of Songtsen Gyampo, was credited with introducing Buddhism to Tibet. In present times, Princess Wencheng had become a potent propaganda tool. She was often promoted as the connection from antiquity between Tibet and China, propaganda that subtly hinted how Buddhism, the essence of Tibetans, and civilization in general, had been a gift from the Han Chinese to the Tibetans. Accordingly, myths associated with Princess Wencheng had grown energetically in modern China. It was rather fashionable to name shops in Tibetan areas—which were typically run by Han Chinese—after Wencheng. In Lhasa, every night when the weather permitted, Wencheng, a 'spectacular' musical of 'epic proportions' with 600 performers, 70 cows and 30 horses, played to massive Han audiences. At the same time, Chinese historians argued over the historical veracity of the existence of Bhrikuti Devi, credited with introducing Buddhism in Tibet. Incidentally, the only temple dedicated to Wencheng was in Kham, in the Yushu prefecture in Qinghai province.

I spent the rest of the day scavenging Kangding's streets for pebbles of the right size. Lobo admonished me for being so suspicious of dogs, a species she had always considered fraternal, part of the primate evolution chain. But I was determined to stock up strategic reserves—and I also needed some practice in pelting stones.

At night, Kangding became an illuminated fairyland as neon lamps in rainbow colours, much appreciated all over China, lit up everything around the two rivers, making the town look like a sin city. Everyone appeared to have come out on the streets, tourists with selfie sticks and locals with their pet dogs. These were small, fluffy, manicured dogs, so different from the Tibetan mastiffs. But wasn't that what practice targets were supposed to be? So whenever I saw one, I would reach for my pockets, but Lobo was on the watch for a situation just like this and the moment we came across a poodle, she would pull me away from the shooting range.

By 7 in the evening, the town square had transformed into a vibrant place. More than 200 people had assembled to dance in circles. The 'Kangding Love Song' blared out of the public speakers as a giant screen played looping videos of the natural wonders of the county. The dancers, mostly women, had organized themselves into three large concentric circles. Men in hats stood in between these circles, attentively observing what was less dance, more calisthenics. I joined the gang of male anthropologists while Lobo joined the dancers. Soon Tibetan pop music replaced the 'Kangding Love Song', but it would reappear every now and then. The Tibetans kept counting their beads while dancing. I was rather pleased to see Hans and Tibetans, young and old, dancing together but soon I realized that each group stuck to each other within the circular formation.

After 30 minutes of dancing, Lobo was tired and happy. The male anthropologists told us that the dancing would continue well until midnight and was a good way for the elderly to stay fit. We went to a restaurant by the square that specialized in 'milk noodles.' Upon hearing that I was from India, the ladies managing the shop couldn't contain their confusion, 'India, are the people there black or are they white? No, no, blacks are the Africans. Your skin is fair.'

Later that night, we went back to the bus station to book a car that could take us to Tagong the next morning. The familiar gang of Tibetan drivers was loitering around so we confirmed a shared van for 50 yuan. The gigabytes of traveller reviews that I had read while planning this trip had made me paranoid about such transactions. Warnings were in the tune of, 'Don't trust a Tibetan driver. They agree on one price and upon reaching the destination, the locals will surround the vehicle and support the driver who will ask for a higher rate. Get them to write down the agreed price on a piece of paper,' said one Western tourist.

In the internet world, there was this general sense of suspicion about the commercialization of tourism in the Tibetan regions, its people being portrayed as ever-ready to take advantage of tourists. Tales fed upon tales of locals always seeking to wrench dollars out of travellers, monks asking for atrocious donations after conducting a split-second ceremony in what begins as a seemingly friendly gesture, and of laymen offering charms, animal skins and antiques at the first encounter with a foreigner. These stories were not coming from Han Chinese but from Western tourists. Reading about the frauds one would come across in Tibet, I had been on a 'I can't be fooled' mode right from the word 'go'. I confirmed the price with the driver four times, until finally, the man lost his patience.

'Don't worry. If I give you my word, I won't budge no matter what happens. I am a Tibetan.'

Five

With the Nomads

The shared van from Kangding to Tagong had more passengers than its maker had ever dreamt it of carrying. But I was thankful for this warmth of humanity that wrapped around me because the temperature dropped as the road climbed up to the 4,300-metre-high Zhe Duo (Windy) Pass. All the passengers in the van were Khampa men in well-worn fluffy jackets. As a familiar saying goes about Tibet's three main regions: U-Tsang has the best religion, Amdo has the best horses and Kham has the best men. Finally, I was shoulder to shoulder with these legends of oriental masculinity.

In her Han-bashing and Tibetan-eulogizing story titled 'The Heart and the Flesh', the writer Chi Li, a Han herself, described the Khampa men as endowed with 'towering height, broad shoulders, slim waists, sturdy long legs, chiselled faces, dark complexions that shone like silk, and a valiant, swinging stride.' In other words, they were top-quality boyfriend material, but for their known habit of never washing their feet.

With their toned faces and broad frames, the younger men in our van looked handsome yet ominous as Khampa men were known to be easily excitable. But once they heard that I was from India, they all touched their chests tenderly, clearly appreciating the Dalai Lama connection.

Once we crossed the pass, the relieved driver put on dance music on the car stereo. The passengers relaxed too and everyone started talking on their phones, informing their relatives that they were alive. The landscape changed; grasslands and softly rolling hills replaced the scraggy white peaks. They went on and on, pockmarked with tiny black spots that we realized were grazing yaks.

Just 10 km from Tagong, where the road forked into two, one for Tagong and one for Litang, our van came to a halt. Our driver had a premonition that another passenger would be coming from the opposite direction. He promised us a wait for a mere 10 minutes, but this time, he didn't keep a Tibetan's word. Ten minutes turned into an hour and beyond. At first, we enjoyed this break and took the opportunity to stretch ourselves in the balmy autumn sun.

But soon we were getting impatient. Our driver was constantly on the phone, checking with the driver of the other van that was supposed to be coming in. Even a mother wouldn't have been so anxious for the arrival of her child. Whenever our driver caught our eye, he gave us a big grin and scratched his bum as a sign of apology. The other passengers, however, appeared unperturbed, crouching comfortably by the roadside, fiddling with rosary beads on one hand and mobile phones on the other. A fellow passenger came up to us, 'Don't worry. Life stops but it picks up again.'

The van appeared eventually after two hours.

Just before we reached Tagong, we passed by the valley of 'Ten Thousand Mani Stones'. For miles, the stones along the banks of the stream accompanying the road had been chalk-marked with holy Tibetan words, a few thousand *Om Mani Padme Hum* mantras. It reminded me of my school days when our teachers asked us to write disciplinary phrases like 'I shall submit homework on time' a thousand times. The biggest tragedy of such a punishment was having to ask my hard-working parents for a new notebook, beyond their annual budget, because the disciplinary phrases would fill up the budgeted one. If only I could have thought like these Tibetans and had scribbled on the school walls instead!

The town of Tagong, located 3,700 metre above sea level, was little more than a town square the size of a soccer field, with a lamasery, a monastery, a handful of guest houses and shops, and a few scattered houses. Without spending any time in Tagong, we left straight for the grasslands, hoping for an encounter with the nomads.

To find our way to the nomads, we had the most enchanting of maps I had used so far—a 300-word written paragraph. Angela Lankford (real name), an American who had settled down with the nomads, had sent me the following instructions in an email:

> **Directions:** Following the red line ... continue straight on the road for five minutes, until the road splits to a large temple, and a bridge, to the right. Go right, and cross this second bridge over the smaller river. Take an immediate right again to head back to the large river. Follow that road as it turns to go up-river (opposite town)... continue walking.... Don't go into the village; continue on the road. Also don't turn left just after the bridge; go straight... You need to find the saddle of the hill; at the bottom the path it is vague or non-existent, but near the top it becomes clear. You must get to the saddle, the lowest crossover point into the next valley! From there, follow the clear horse trail ...

I read this again and again as if memorizing them would remove any confusion. We couldn't even find the starting point —the red line.

We took a guess and followed our shadows. And soon, all the sentences in Angela's description began falling into place. Dogs followed us for a while without appearing to be threatening and after we reached the side valley, there was no sign of humanity. A dirt track, a narrow stream, gentle hills covered with scruffy grass, blue skies, cold winds and a bright sun; it seemed to go on forever.

And then there were the yaks, scattered over the landscape in huge numbers. They were curious animals, looking at us with deep questioning eyes. The younger ones gave us a chase till their mothers called them back (herds mostly comprised females and baby yaks as grown-up males tend to remain solitary). Despite their majestic size, their coarse shaggy bodies made the yaks look like backbenchers from school. From time to time, they shed all the grace in the world to lie down on their backs and roll around in a pit to get a lovely scratch.

As these mountain queens looked at us, I felt like an intruder in their world, a realm the yaks had adapted so well to. To cope with thin mountain air, they had oversized hearts and lungs, and three times the number of blood cells as compared to a normal cow. Their thick hair, skin secretions, and a bowel that constantly worked at a high temperature, helped them survive the cold up to altitudes of 6,000 metre. But, despite all such bodily tricks, wild yaks have almost disappeared from the earth. Their greatest adaptation had been to become domesticated and ask little from their human masters.

Tibetans, in return—at least the Khams we met along the way—claimed that they never slaughtered the yaks and were not even allowed to sell their yaks to butchers. When I asked about all the yak meat on the restaurant menus, they would say that the meat was from those yaks which died naturally or from unfortunate events, such as falling off a cliff. A yak's lifespan was only 20 years; yet, judging from the abundance of yak meat in restaurants and butcher shops, there must be many of them falling off from the cliffs every day!

After two hours of walking, we had to get off the dirt track and look for the saddle in the hill according to Angela's instructions. As we began climbing, our backpacks began to make their presence felt. The sun was fierce and the air was thin. Both of us developed headaches and a general sense of hopelessness. The saddle was moving further and further away from us. Lobo sat down every five steps and whenever she rested, she babbled nonsense with her head bobbing like a pigeon. All this while, the yaks kept munching with a 'Who told you to come?' look. After an arduous hour of climbing, we finally reached the saddle and out of nowhere, the snow-covered Yala Mountain appeared on the horizon.

Yala revived our spirits. At 5,820 metre, Yala was a relative minnow in the Hengduan Mountains system, the mountain range that connects the Tibetan Plateau with the Yunnan–Guizhou Plateau in southwest China. But in the grasslands of Tagong, Yala dominated its surroundings. Looking like an inverted cupcake foil contrasted by a clear blue sky and the sunburnt grassland all around, this was one of the most beautiful mountains I had ever seen.

We ran down the slopes while photographing the mountain incessantly—framed by a red bush, then with a bunch of yaks in the foreground, then with the clear blue stream, then against a white tent. White tent! We had entered the world of the nomads.

It was approaching sunset, but our destination was still far. With Yala to our back, Lobo and I prodded along like zombies. To make things easier, I took the grave risk of emptying my pockets of the stones I had brought along to counterattack dogs. With 5 kg less, the journey became a little more tolerable. Completely exhausted, we finally reached Angela's house. The three-hour trek had taken us five long hours.

After allowing us some time to rest, Angela clapped and screamed in the direction of a white tent on the slopes on the other side of the river. A Tibetan woman and her baby girl came out and began waving at us. They were saying something in Tibetan that we couldn't understand.

Angela said, 'They are asking you to walk across the river.'

I had always fancied the idea of crossing a river by walking over it. I imagined that a few hundred kilometres down, every mountain stream became a beast like the Mekong or the Salween and crossing it as if I was just going to the neighborhood grocer was my way of conquering Hercules. In the Mustang region of Nepal, on the route from Muktinath to Jomsom, I even did the lunatic act of trying to build a bridge over the gurgling Kali Gandaki River on a full moon night. Lobo had joined me in that implausible effort to carry over large rocks and drop them into the mighty river.

We took off our shoes and socks, and crossed that nameless river in Tagong cumbersomely, holding each other's hands, shrieking whenever the rocks moved beneath our feet. But the flow of the cold water around my legs rid me off all the symptoms of altitude sickness. Once on the other bank, the mother and the daughter waited patiently as we took 20 minutes to fastidiously wipe out every hint of moisture from our feet. When I finally raised my head, what I saw was the big bright smile of the baby girl. She grabbed my hand and we walked together towards the tent. The mother held Lobo's hand.

Inside, the tent appeared larger than it looked from outside. At the centre was the pole that held up the tent. Much of the family's belongings, heaped up like bundles of clothes, were leaning against it. At the far-left corner there was a small tent, a tent within a tent. The father and a toddler were peeking out from the dozen layers of colourful mattresses placed inside this. To the near left of the tent entrance, there was a big vat and other kitchen items. Gunny bags were lined up along this edge, containing stored grains and potatoes. The right quarter of the tent had been ring-fenced and 10 yak babies were tethered behind it. Just next to the entrance, an old Tibetan mastiff was resting. There was a general messiness about the whole place but just outside the tent, Yala Mountain was visible in its sunset glory.

Tibetan tents come in two forms. One is a black tent, woven from yak hair, which is the traditional abode of the nomads. The other is a white tent made of canvas, which is lighter, faster to set up and dismantle, and easier to move around during the nomads' seasonal migrations. Yet, many nomad families continued living in black tents to avoid the expenses of buying a new one. Ours was a white tent.

Our hosts, Tashi and Sonam, were 37 and 39 years old, respectively. Their daughter was called Pema and the son was named Norbu. The couple had another six-year-old boy named Sangyal. Pema was eight and was the oldest child in the family, while Norbu was born only six months ago. Sangyal stayed away from the family in a nearby village where he attended school. The whole family had sharp features, coarse hair and a skin tone darker than the Tibetans we had met so far.

Tashi turned on a small solar lamp and set about preparing for dinner. She had worked in a restaurant in Tagong for a few years and therefore, could speak basic Mandarin. The other members of the family spoke only Tibetan.

Tashi briefed us on the day in the life of a nomad. She said, 'We wake up at six to milk the yaks. We have some light breakfast at seven and then another meal at ten in the morning. During the day, I make butter and cheese from the milk. My husband goes to Tagong sometimes to buy and sell things. He also takes the yaks out for grazing and brings them back in the evening. We have one more meal at three in the afternoon before having dinner at seven. After cleaning up, we sleep by nine.'

Pema wanted to play with me. Since the poor girl didn't have any toys, we played a game of making scary faces at each other. I delighted her immensely by distorting my eyelids, exposing my canines, and putting on the most grimacing face I could manage. We went on like this for a long time, the skill being in bringing subtle variations in each expression.

Dinner was ready in an hour. Each one of us got one tingmo or steamed bun. We were also offered butter, cheese and chilli paste, with mild tea for drinks. The bun looked rather small, making me wonder whether I would stay awake in hunger all night in this cold grassland. I was sure Lobo was thinking the same. We were just being our true urban selfish selves. Surprisingly, it took merely two bites of one mean tingmo to fill up my stomach all the way up to my throat. I finished my bowl of tea to get the third bite down, but more than half of the tingmo mocked me from the bowl. I tried taking smaller and smaller bites of the tingmo. But once inside, these morsels were undergoing a strange chemical transformation to become massive foam pillows. I couldn't quit either for this was precious food for our hosts that they couldn't afford to waste. I persevered.

'Isn't the food too simple?' Tashi asked. She had worked in a restaurant, after all. 'I am so sorry. Can I offer you one more tingmo?'

To be the perfect hostess, Tashi put a few more dough balls in the pan for steaming. I wanted to scream, 'Stop!' but the sound ricocheted off the tingmo stuffed into my throat.

It was only seven by the time we finished dinner. All this while, Sonam had been sitting quietly with Norbu on his lap. Since he didn't speak any Mandarin, he couldn't talk to us. He had also been suffering from fever for a few days.

'The nearest doctor is in Tagong,' Tashi said. 'He is not in a state to ride his motorcycle and go there.'

I offered them some antipyretics, which they accepted gratefully. Sonam consumed them immediately and went to sleep with Norbu.

Tashi settled the dishes by just throwing out the leftover liquids inside the tent and wiping off the bowls with her hands. That triggered wide-eyed horror from our Singapore-conditioned hypersensitivity about sanitization. It was hard to keep the tent clean with every facet of family life happening within that small area.

Then there were the baby yaks, which had been urinating and excreting continuously. With the strong sun, the cold of the night, and the general lack of fruits and vegetables in the diet, it was an easy place to fall sick in. Birth complications (from unsterilized conditions), urinary problems, hepatitis, tuberculosis, arthritis, gallbladder disease, peptic ulcers and back pain were relatively common among nomads.[4] Life expectancy for the whole of Tibet had improved from 35.5 years in 1951 to 67 years in 2010, but that for the nomads was around 46.[5]

After dinner, Tashi told us that she had met Sonam at a festival in Tagong. 'There were more than 150 people who came for my wedding. My husband had to pay for the feast and for everything else.'

She showed us her two gold teeth and giggled like a young girl, 'I got these at my wedding. All Tibetan women must have these.'

Tashi was curious about how Lobo and I got married and wanted to know who paid for the expenses and how many people attended. What gifts did Lobo get?

Then she asked Lobo, 'Where are your gold teeth?'

Both polyandry and polygamy were prevalent among the nomads, but it was practised mostly under the condition that if more than one partner of the same sex was involved, they were all from the same family. Polyandry and polygamy were perhaps solutions to prevent any break-up of herds and pastoral land into unviable lots. However, in modern times, when birth rates have fallen drastically, this practice was also on the wane. Tashi and Sonam had no other partners.

After their wedding, Sonam moved in to live with Tashi's community. This group of nomad families, about 50 of them, had perhaps been together for over a thousand years. This was not unusual in Tibet where nomad groups stuck to each other and moved together. Moving was one of the biggest decisions for nomads because it involved considerable effort. The group, therefore, decided collectively on each such move.

'Winter is the hardest time for us,' Tashi told us. 'The yaks can only eat dry grass then. But that is not enough and it gets less and less as winter wears on. Many yaks die during winter. In winter, we come down to lower elevations, next to rivers and streams. In the past, we used to build sod dugouts, but they barely lasted a few seasons because the grass we used to construct them wore out quickly. Now, we build brick and cement houses.'

Yet, even today, winter could bring peril for the nomads. During extended periods of snowstorms, remote herds could get cut off for weeks from larger settlements. Then the clock of death would start ticking.

'If someone is lost for a few days, the yaks die first,' said Tashi. 'If a yak dies, the man will die too if he can't come back in time. Sometimes a son dies in front of his father.'

In that sense, the lives of the nomads in Tibet were no different from that of the Bedouins in the deserts of Arabia and North Africa where a whole family could perish because of the death of one camel.

'But even during summer, nomads can die suddenly because when it rains heavily, sometimes people are struck by lightning.'

Life as a nomad is especially hard for the elderly who give in to exposure faster. In the past, the elderly nomads used to stay in tents with their families until they died. Nowadays, most nomads wanted their elderly relatives to move to a nearby temple, once they had reached the age of 55–60.

Pema dragged me away from the conversation. It was time to play 'geography-geography'. She dug a few matchsticks on to the soil to mark the important landmarks—her tent, Tagong and Kangding. She made her fingers walk from her tent to Tagong and Kangding and then back, biting her teeth with happiness every time she finished the trip. Pema had never been to school despite the government making education mandatory. She did not even know how to count. But she was the liveliest and most adorable child I had ever known. The tent was at once the happiest place on earth and the most miserable too.

As the conversation waned, Lobo suggested we play cards. We tried to teach them rummy but Tashi just froze. Thinking they were not good with numbers, we started a colour-matching card game but Tashi remained frozen. We relented, guessing that she took the cards as a symbol of unholy gambling. Pema was already dozing off, so Tashi commanded us, 'Let's also sleep.'

Tashi assembled our bed by unfolding mattresses on the sloping ground between the central pole and the entrance. Then she placed layer upon layer of stiff blankets, some made of wool, some of leather.

'It gets really cold,' she said. 'You will need all of this.'

Pema kicked the old dog, their pet, out of the tent.

'This dog is so lazy,' laughed Tashi. 'He should keep watch at night like the dogs in other families but he keeps coming in to sleep.'

Once I got underneath the blankets, I felt like I had been buried alive under their massive weight.

Yet it felt cosy. Tashi turned off the solar lamp and everything became quiet, except for the burbling stream outside. But there were the baby yaks which called out intermittently for their mothers after every bad dream. Soon, the dog sneaked back in and lay curled up next to my feet. But I didn't feel the need to reach out for my stones. Experiencing this pastoral life, I was happy at the contentedness of that moment, although I knew that I would be out of there the next day.

Around midnight, Sonam began to cough. He coughed and coughed and coughed. Lobo woke up and began to panic.

'I hope we don't catch the infection from him,' she whispered to me.

Cough... cough... cough...

'We shouldn't fall sick.'

Cough... cough... cough...

'I don't want to fall sick. It's so early in the trip.'

Even louder cough.

'We will fall sick! Take me out of here, please.'

I explained to her that out of here was a stream and the Yala Mountain.

She tossed and turned.

Coughs from hell.

'We will die. We will die here.' She was not whispering any more.

A long-stretched cough that might have thrown Sonam's entrails out of his throat went on.

Lobo began sobbing.

I rubbed her back and tried to console her. I explained that the situation would be better one day, even for us. I told her that the clinic at Tagong was just a few hours away and made up some scientific-sounding facts about low aerial rates of transmission for infectious diseases.

Hearing my soothing voice, a baby yak moaned and took a piss. Lobo laughed and began to calm down. Sonam calmed down as well. But the yak's loud pissing drew in a reflex urge in me to urinate. I dreaded venturing out of the tent in the freezing cold. It was now my turn to panic. I began to toss and turn. Lobo saw my stress and tried to pacify me by rubbing my back. Once I explained the situation, she made a decision,

'Let's go. We will manage.'

I shoved the dog aside and quietly, we sneaked out of the tent. It was cold yet pleasant. We found sheltered spots to pee and once settled, I looked up at the sky to see a perfect vision of the Milky Way. I had never seen so many stars, clearly outnumbering the dark spaces between them. Lobo and I snuggled up to each other as we sat down on the ground.

As insignificant as we were, I was glad to be able to observe this spectacle of nature, this enormous beauty that had sprung from that most ancient of explosions, so imperfect and yet so perfect, an incomparable phenomenon that even at its age of 13.6 billion years, made me gasp and choke in wonder. The stream, the yaks relaxing on their beloved grass, the family back in the tent who practised the most primitive of lifestyles and the universe in all its glory over us—it was too overwhelming.

It could have been an hour, or two, or longer. We just sat there and dissolved into the magic around us. At some point, the old mastiff came out and began to bark. He must have been feeling cold without my feet to curl against. Or perhaps, he was doing his job and had smelled a wolf that roamed in these valleys. We went back in, followed by the dog.

Tashi and Sonam woke up before sunrise. Sonam was feeling a lot better and thanked us profusely for the medicines. Tashi prepared a breakfast of zanba, the Tibetan staple of roasted barley powder. She filled up our bowls from the previous night and showed us how to eat the zanba by making a hole in the centre of the serving with a finger, putting in some yak butter and hot water, stirring it around to make small agglutinated chunks, after which one could eat these dough balls. Once again, it was food hard to swallow. Tashi licked the edges of the bowl like a cat to finish off all the zanba and prodded us to do the same.

Sonam left soon for the pastures. Tashi untied one of the baby yaks. Once freed, its first reaction was to run over to me and head-butt me.

Tashi laughed out loud, 'They do that to their mothers when they are hungry. This one is still too young and thinks you are its mother.'

The sun was rising and Yala Mountain was bright red, framed by the dark silhouettes of yak horns. A thin layer of fog covered the grasslands.

Tashi began calling out, *'Aley, blik blik blik blik blik blik ... aley, blik blik blik blik blik blik...'*

Suddenly, Pema appeared on the horizon, chasing a yak towards us. Once the mother yak came closer, Tashi walked in between us and the yak, 'Mothers get aggressive easily,' she explained.

Tashi tied the mother's hind legs so she couldn't kick and allowed the head-butting baby to start drinking milk. After it was satisfied, Tashi began milking the mother.

'We have 30 yaks,' said Tashi. 'We collect a bucketful of milk each day but during summer we can collect a lot more.'

She looked happy and contented. Tilting her head against a yak's legs, she began humming a song.

Since Tashi could speak only limited Mandarin, I would later discuss nomadic life with experts in Sichuan (whose names cannot be revealed) as well as read through available research on this topic. What I learnt was that nomadic life, which was very much about sustenance in the past, had become more business-like with China's economic growth. Historically, the yaks (in some cases, sheep) were all the nomads had to survive. The yaks provided the staple foods—milk, butter and cheese. Yak dung was used as fuel and yak hair for making black tents. But these families also needed to buy salt, barley and tea from the markets which they paid for by selling yak products, mostly butter, but also dried skimmed cheese, hides, fibre and then meat when yaks died 'accidentally'. But as prices and access to markets had improved, a typical Kham nomad family made about 30,000 to 40,000 yuan a year (US$4,500-6,000), about half to two-thirds of which came from yak products. The rest came from selling caterpillar fungus, a recent entry to the Chinese pantheon of fad health supplements and a boon for Tibetans. Some Kham nomads cut and sold Sichuan Baimu (cypress) wood. Nomads in other areas also collected and sold matsutake mushrooms. The poorer nomads, however, those with less than 10 yaks, still lived at the border of sustenance.

As we were preparing to leave, Angela's daughter dropped by from across the river. Born in Colorado, Angela had always been a mountain woman. She had come to China as a Peace Corps staff member and once she met her husband, a Tibetan man, she decided to stay on.

'I moved over here once I realized how important family relationships were in my husband's culture,' she had told us earlier.

Angela maintained a website that sold arts and crafts from Kham nomads, such as woven blankets and curtains, garments, metal items and jewellery.

'I am always doing new projects. The first one was Khampa Café and Arts Centre in Tagong. Now, I am building this eco-house here.'

'I don't miss the modern world,' she had said. 'I have everything here. Even for healthcare, if some sophisticated treatment is required, the airport is just 45 minutes away. And I don't miss the supermarkets because those are just big collections of one chemical food after another. Isn't that true?'

But things couldn't be that simple in this remote and harsh landscape. A few months later, Angela's dog died and I saw a sad note from her. She lamented that it was a simple infection that could have been cured by a vet, only if there had been one available nearby or if she herself had been a vet.

Angela's daughter was being home-schooled. Angela had said, 'I can't imagine my daughter growing up in the United States, in Colorado. It's too white a place.'

That set me wondering about where Lobo and I could raise our children if ever we had any. Could it be China or India, countries where Lobo and I came from respectively, with their ever-increasing prevalence of mind-numbing exclusivist nationalistic storylines, or could it be Singapore, with its ever-tentative sterility, cocooned away from the exalting freedom of a steppe, the exotic simplicity of untamed Gauguinesqe tropics, or the neuron-dense complexity of possibilities in an African slum?

As we said goodbye, I knew I would miss Pema, who had become a friend with whom I didn't need to know any language but just understand what fun was all about. Would Pema's life be any different from her mother's? I didn't know because life for Tibetan nomads—unchanged for thousands of years—had undergone big swings in the last 50 years. The arrival of the Communist government brought in negligible changes in the initial years but massive disruption came in the wake of the collectivization of pastoral life and the destruction of the official power of the monasteries just before and during the Cultural Revolution.

During the early years of Deng Xiaoping's rule as the leader of the People's Republic of China, the rights to the land and the animals were given back to the individual nomad families. Around 2006, the Chinese government significantly expanded an earlier programme of relocating Tibetan nomads into fixed settlements under the 'Opening of the West' initiative, during which they also fenced in the nomads' pastures and asked them to form cooperatives, the official goal being to help raise living standards and protect the environment. Houses and electricity were provided for free or were heavily subsidized as billions of dollars were pumped into the project.

Tibetan exiles and foreign human rights organizations, however, protested that the nomads were being relocated forcibly and this was merely

an excuse to free up land for mining and other
commercial activities. The truth, as always, perhaps
lay somewhere in between. But I was realizing soon
that in the charged rhetorical world of Tibetan issues,
where both parties aggressively projected their side
of stories and histories, it was nearly impossible to
locate that 'somewhere in between'.

During 2012–13, many Kham nomads sold off their
herds and moved to towns, though not necessarily into
the government settlement projects which remained
largely empty. This was when the economy of western
China was in full bloom, driven by mega-investments
by the government in infrastructure projects. Those
who left included poor families with few yaks whose
life in the grasslands was anyway marginal.

Many wealthy nomads left too, those who had
already made enough money through various
unrelated businesses (furniture, real estate, black
market activities) and whose women saw little point
continuing with the hard pastoral work to earn a
negligible part of their family income. Some were
people running away from feuds, while others were
just young people who sought something new.

The towns, however, turned out to be disappointing
as the economy slowed down all too soon. Nomads
found that the towns demanded skills rather
different from what they possessed and much of the
trading had already been taken over by the Hans.
Most importantly, their education was below par
for what the market needed. Women felt that they
would rather work with yaks than just stay at home

with the children. The nomads, who had come to consider abundant milk, butter and cheese a free gift from nature, were confounded when they had to pay for the same in town markets. Not only was food unaffordable, but it was also inferior to what they used to make in their tents. Soon, many turned back to their pastures. Those who stayed back were mostly the elderly, or families with newborn babies. Even the young returned to the grasslands to become nomads, rejecting the 'Chinese Life'.

Six

Back to Tagong

I struggled on the way back. We had taken a different route and Tagong always appeared too close and yet too far. Every 10 minutes, I had to drop my backpack and rest. Nomads, who passed by on motorcycles, offered us a ride, but we were two and with the backpacks, we were as good as four. I walked like a zombie. All my preparations for high-altitude trekking, such as daily running up 2,000 stairs in Singapore, did not help me much. Lobo, who had undertaken no such preparation, was doing fine.

After two hours of walking, I gave up and lay down on the grassland. I dozed off despite the highland sun being full on my face. Only later would I get to know that Tibetans forbade sleeping in the open because they believed that mountain spirits kidnapped such people or took away their eyesight.

When I woke up, Lobo was talking to a Tibetan mastiff that was 10 steps away. Startled, I reached for the nearest stones. But Lobo, the all-weather dog lover, grabbed my wrist to stop me, saying, 'It's friendly'.

Suddenly, I hit upon the next Alibaba idea. If Lobo could befriend this brute and convince it to follow us, we could make a killing by selling it to Chinese tourists in Tagong. Tibetan mastiffs had become status symbols for China's rich who had already bought all the Lamborghinis and Guccis produced by humanity, and needed something new to tell their tale. These dogs then made it to their list of must-have items, fetching prices as high as 1.6 million dollars.[6] But when the economy slowed and the government sniffed for evidences of corruption, prices crashed and many owners offloaded their mastiffs for sale as hotpot meat. It was still possible to get up to US$10,000 for one such dog. The dog in our line of sight looked far from being a status symbol. Yet, wouldn't we be able to smooth-talk a gullible tourist and get a hundred dollars for this golden goose? And we could come back to the grasslands to do this again and again. A disruptive business model with guaranteed revenues that disintermediated conventional mastiff breeding oligopolies, was a proposal that should get Silicon Valley's angel investors drooling.

So when we started moving again, I sang all the lullabies I knew and even dangled a biscuit in front of the dog's eyes. But this dullard just wouldn't budge. I was certain that he smirked at me before he went chasing a dragonfly. So be it, you frog in the well, live your life getting kicked out of nomad tents. Anyway, it had been one great roller-coaster ride—from start-up ideas to nothing, all within a space of five minutes.

Once we reached Tagong, we headed straight for Khampa Café to have a change of taste after the authentic Tibetan fare with the nomads. Khampa Café was started by Angela who then sold it to Max, a young Czech. Max had travelled all around China and then settled down at Tagong with his girlfriend who was from the nearby valley of Danba. A man who seemed to be so much in love with this place also had a lot of complaints about it.

'Everything is so expensive here,' he said. 'Like you spend so much on a chicken and then there's hardly any meat in it.' He went on, 'There comes the garbage man. He is a celebrity. The most popular sport in Tagong is to run when the garbage man arrives because he disappears in a flash.'

'I wouldn't recommend cycling here. Tibetans drive like maniacs. And Chinese tourists don't see what they are doing while driving.'

'Nothing much to see in Danba. Nothing much to see in Litang. Why would I want to live in Lhasa? It's just another Chinese town.'

But on one point, I agreed wholeheartedly with him, about the monotony of Sichuan food.

'Yes, you are right,' he said. 'It is always the same flavour—Sichuan pepper and chilli. And Tibetan food is too bland. I much prefer Indian food.'

In the spirit of India, Max prepared two large cups of masala tea for us. It was delightful indeed. Max drew final blood, 'Some Tibetans here who had gone to study in India say that Indian food is not nice. To them, I can only say—hey!'

We checked into a Tibetan guest house where the interiors had been painted densely with colourful motifs of birds, animals and Tibetan symbols. It seemed like the work of a child who had an endless supply of paints but only one copybook to paint upon. This dreamy fairyland imagery made us sleep a good six hours during the day to make up for the previous night. In the evening, we explored the lamasery and the monastery in Tagong. A lot of Chinese tourists, mostly from Sichuan, visited the temples. We talked to Mr Wang, an enthusiastic photographer who seemed to enjoy every crack and corner in the Tagong monastery. As most Chinese did, Mr Wang also spoke in superlatives.

'This monastery is one of the best. Look, there is so much gold. And nobody takes any of it off. This is why Tibet is so special. They are not like us, only after money.'

The Tagong monastery did have some reputation. It was arguably built by the same Princess Wencheng whose statue we had seen in Kangding. She chose this spot because on her way to Lhasa to get married to King Songtsen Gyampo, she had accidentally dropped the statue of Jowo (Sakyamuni Buddha) at Tagong. Mr

Wang had said, 'This statue is no ordinary statue. It came from your India, a gift from some Magadha king to the Chinese emperor.'

The original statue resided at the famed Jokhang temple in Lhasa and was of utmost importance to Tibetans. Its replica could be viewed in Tagong. 'This monastery gets thousands of Tibetan pilgrims every winter, maybe millions,' Mr Wang had said. 'Thousands of Hans also come here. Maybe millions. Not just from China, even from Southeast Asia and America.'

But while more and more Hans were getting attracted to Tibetan Buddhism, they largely avoided displaying any reverence for the Dalai Lama. Such an attitude was probably the outcome of the decades-old propaganda unleashed by the Chinese government against the Dalai Lama, every mention of whose name in the official media was invariably accompanied with qualifiers such as 'cheater', 'cruel ruler in exile', 'violent separatist', 'a small figure' and the most popular, 'a wolf in monk's robes' and 'a wolf in sheep's clothing'.[7]

As we walked back to the Tagong square, a young man in a motorbike stopped for an impromptu chat with us. He was a nomad from Aba County in northern Sichuan who had come to Tagong to trade. He had a brief talk with us and as he departed, he said, 'Let me tell you that I like you Han people. I have nothing against them. Some Han people are good and some are bad just like everyone else.'

That was rather out of context and I was not a Han.

Yet we did not question his argument. People from Aba were known to be the most easily excitable among Tibetans. In the recent past, Aba had also witnessed the highest number of self-immolations in opposition to what protesters termed the 'Han occupation'. Incidentally, both the monastery and the lamasery discreetly displayed portraits of the Dalai Lama. A few years back, such behaviour would not have been permitted by the government of China.

As the sun went down, stalls selling yak yoghurt sprouted up along the roadside, just like in Chengdu. The souvenir shopkeepers called out to us and Lobo bought some Tibetan trinkets for herself. Then she had the bright idea to buy more trinkets, for the babies scheduled to be born to her friends this year. Then she had a brighter idea of buying some more trinkets—for those babies of friends that were yet to be in the planning stage! Once inside my bag, all these trinkets jingled, forming an orchestra that made passers-by wonder if I was the reincarnation of a heavily belled yak.

Back at our guest house, we sat for a while in the lobby because that was the only place where the internet was available. The room was actually the sleeping area for the only staff at that place. The middle-aged Tibetan man was watching television and didn't look pleased at our invasion. It did not take long to understand why, as it was a steamy Chinese movie where a gang of scantily clad supermodels killed male targets one by one. But within a few minutes, he and I formed some sort of male bonding as both of us cheered, in a rather dignified way, after each successful execution.

Seven

The World's Highest Town

White crane!
Lend me your wings
I will not fly far
From Litang, I shall return.

—Tsangyang Gyatso, the Sixth Dalai Lama

In western Sichuan, the travel industry has its own subculture. To travel from town A to town B, one has to arrive at A's town square just after sunrise. That's where and when van drivers assemble, looking for passengers. It is almost impossible to travel the same day if one appears at the square after 9 a.m. Early in the morning, these van drivers, Tibetan men with a lot of flair and robust sense of humour, kept calling out the names of towns: Litang, Litang, Litang..., Kangding, Kangding, Kangding....'

If one asked to go to Xinduchao instead, these drivers would immediately change their calls: 'Xinduchao, Xinduchao, Xinduchao....'

If one driver had already been approached by a prospective passenger, she would not be targeted by the other drivers. From that point onwards, it was a game of patience and luck. The driver would start only if there was a quorum of passengers going to the same place. That could take 10 minutes in the best of days and in smaller towns, a week.

For Litang, we could only get a shared car up to Xinduchao, from where we would have to change. As soon as our car reached Xinduchao, we were rushed along by the local drivers.

'There is only one seat available for Litang,' said one of them. 'Hurry, hurry.'

'But we are two people,' Lobo said.

'That's what we are saying,' the driver said. 'You have to hurry before another person comes in.'

The initial stretch of the road from Xinduchao to Litang was a script written for nightmares, but something we had gotten used to by now. After an hour of shared agony in this shared van, the pockmarked road became an unexpected smooth wonder and then a sheer delight as we passed by valleys dotted with tiny Tibetan villages, their smart homes looking similar to those in the arid towns of North Africa with roofs shaped like Dilbert's head, jagged triangles on a square base. Another van accompanied us throughout this trip and every now and then the drivers made us swap places between the two vans, as if they were working on a complicated problem of load balancing, never quite getting it right. After a few such iterations, we were left with only one other passenger in a van that could accommodate nine while the other van was filled chock-a-block. Whatever the logic for this redistribution might have been, our ride became immensely enjoyable as we were soon surrounded by snow-covered peaks. Yet, the sense of danger persisted because our driver kept getting calls while we crossed one high pass after another. When we asked him to be more careful, he showed us his wedding picture on his mobile phone.

'That's the person I am talking to,' he said. 'Isn't she beautiful? She keeps calling me because she is worried whenever I take this route.'

Lobo told the driver, 'Let me also talk to her and tell her that if she really loves you, she should please stop calling.'

After five hours of driving, we saw Litang, nestled in a mossy valley surrounded by gentle snowy peaks on all sides. As we got down, our drivers and fellow passengers wished us all the best for our travels.

'Come, let us also take a photograph together with

our Indian friend,' our driver said.

'It will cost 100 yuan for one photo,' I demanded.

He hugged me, sneaked in his arms through mine and posed, 'I don't make that much in one week. Just do it for free for a friend.'

I felt sad parting with them. I didn't know if I would ever take this road again, but these hardened drivers had to pass through these deadly paths every day. When I had just arrived, I had been suspicious of Tibetans since the internet articles had put me on guard against their reported wiles. But as I got to know them better, their kindness, openness, truthfulness, curiosity and sense of humour had endeared them to me. Travelling was working on my mind just as it should.

Litang was a construction site, with a long history. The roads in the town were all dug up. A thick blanket of dust shrouded the town, almost blinding people who walked carefully, somehow avoiding the countless open manholes. The shutters of all the shops were down, their locks gathering rust. It was a town listening to its own version of the Tibetan Book of the Dead, a constant screeching noise of shovels and spades working on wet cement. We had arrived before the town had the time to be reincarnated.

Indeed, Litang was the town for reincarnations. Among Tibetans, the odds of being selected to be a very senior Tibetan monk was the highest if one was born in Litang, with the usual disclaimer about past performance not being indicative of the future. The reincarnations of the Sixth and the Ninth Dalai Lamas were born in Litang, so were four of the Pabalas (Living Buddhas resident in Chamdo monastery), and a series of leading Tulkus (another lineage of Living Buddhas). When we asked our drivers from Tagong about what made Litang such a special place, one had joked, 'Because Litang is at such a great height. Anyone who can survive here is already a gifted person.'

Located at an altitude of 13,000 feet, Litang boldly claimed to be the highest town in the world. This claim was memorized by the local establishments who then spat it out like a compulsively obsessed parrot, with every billboard and shopfront signboard shouting 'World's High Town' or 'Global Highest Town'.

Litang was also a town of strange English translations. In a country infamous for its interpretation of the English language, that indeed stood for something. We got tired taking pictures of these aphorisms: 'Snowfall science and technology museum', 'Non-staple food shops', 'Horse riding friend stage hotel', 'Noodle coup shop', 'Geopolitical hairdressing shop', 'Brother wide vegetable store'. Although they made perfect sense before, gradually, they did not.

We checked in to a hotel run by someone called 'Longlife'. 'Longlife' was a kind of internet celebrity in the Western world without him knowing it, as many travel blogs mentioned him as the person to go to for arranging any trip in western Sichuan. These bloggers invariably emphasized his name 'Longlife' but in reality it was just a literal translation of a very common Tibetan name, 'Tsering'.

As in other Asian cultures, Tibetan names either correspond to good human qualities, such as 'noble' (Lobsang) or 'resolute' (Rabten), or well-meaning words, such as 'long life' and 'auspicious' (Tashi). There are also names, such as 'messenger of dharma' (Chodak) and 'thunderbolt' (Dorje), names that exemplify a very Tibetan way of life. Tibetan names are gender-neutral although some names are more common among either sex. A peculiar if not confusing aspect is that even though Tibetan names typically comprise two words, there is no concept of a family name; the two names being just glorious words that in combination create an awesome effect (however, in the past, some Tibetan aristocrats did have family names and these days many commoners have created family names for themselves). Sometimes, a part of the name was just the day on which the child was born.

When a child is born in a Tibetan household, the family assigns him or her a provisional name while waiting for a reincarnated lama to give a formal name. It has become fashionable to send such a request straight to the Dalai Lama now. Even deep into adulthood, if a person happens to meet an esteemed lama, it is not unusual to request for a new name. Some Tibetans follow the Chinese practice of giving a grotesque name, such as Khikyag (dog shit), hoping that this would protect the child from the evil eye, particularly if the family had lost a child before. At the same time, names which appeared too similar to Hans, such as Ling or Yangchen, were consciously avoided or adopted, depending on the political attitude of the family.

Famous personalities such as the Dalai Lamas, legendary Tibetan saints and the three Dharma kings provided inspiration for most names. So during our trip, I had a feeling that I was constantly meeting alter egos of the same people—Tenzin or Songtsen. This was a practical problem and rumour had it that many people worked for years in government jobs that had actually been offered to someone else. Han schoolteachers, in particular, struggled with this and there was an abundant collection of hilarious tales of a certain Milarepa's parents being warned about another Milarepa's follies.

The hotels were getting cheaper as we got deeper into Kham but the views were getting better. In Litang, our large window opened up to a gallery of snowy peaks. But we couldn't enjoy this for long as the strong sunlight forced us to draw the curtains soon. Many songs about Litang praised the town for its blue skies and bright sunlight. For this reason, people in Litang loved to dry clothes. All day, we could see the rooftops of Litang occupied by Kung-fu women swinging around with flowing cloth, hanging one bedsheet on one line and then swirling to hang a mattress on to another, then a swift dash in light steps with an undergarment to the next available sunny spot and then back to where they had started with a scarf.

In the evening, we went to the white pagoda on the outskirts of Litang. The prayer wheel inside the temple there was unbelievably large—20 metre high and 10 metre across—and was rotating fast. It was like Jupiter with all her moons, the humans who held on to the orbital rim of the prayer wheel and circumambulated around it. Just before the entrance to this giant cyclotron, nuns and other devotees were doing prostrations. As anyone who had taken a gym lesson would know, a prostration—a burpee as it is known in gym lingo—is one of the most efficient exerises that combines both aerobics and anaerobics. I could do only 20 burpees at one go, but these nuns went on and on. Lobo joined them and gave up at the count of three.

Once inside, we joined the orbit of the praying wheel. It was actually being operated by an electrical motor and not by human power. There were many children, some mere toddlers who walked around in clumsy steps. There were many elderly people too, wearing cowboy hats, boots and many layers of shawls, who lumbered along with bent backs. I was drawing attention because of my standout appearance. One by one they approached Lobo, handed their phones to her and asked her to take a photograph of them with me. At one point in this queue for my pictures, we encountered a woman called Tsering who had brought along her pre-teen daughter. Tsering could speak Mandarin and upon hearing that I was from India, she couldn't control her emotions.

'Come, child,' she told her daughter. 'Touch him. He is from India where our Dalai Lama resides.'

Tsering held my hands and touched her forehead with them. 'Oh, I am so glad to meet you. You are from the land where he walks now.'

She was weeping. 'You can see our Dalai Lama, but we can't. Please go and visit him once and tell him about us.'

It was moving for me as well. It was not that the Dalai Lama was staying at my house. And yet, such was the power of religion that this negligible association was significant for these people.

Tsering's histrionics drew a bigger crowd around me again. Everyone wanted a picture. Once the interest ebbed, I attempted a conversation and asked the gathering about the significance of the stupa.

'Let's ask the master,' said a novice monk who looked like an endearing village fool. 'I am only a novice.'

He dragged me to a chubby monk who had been watching us all along from a distance. Mr Village Fool look-alike asked the monk, 'Tell him something good from Buddhism, teacher. He is from India.'

The monk looked disinterested, like a child who has ceased to be the centre of attention in a family that was playing host to guests with their children. He avoided making eye contact with me and spoke only to Lobo. 'What is there to tell you?' he asked. 'This place is closing down now.'

He spoke anyway, 'Well, there is this white stupa here, a black stupa in Xinduchao and a coloured one in Kham. All three were built by Princess Wencheng.'

'We circle around the stupa three times—the first circle is for good karma, second for the spirits, third for world peace. Are you happy? Have I answered all your questions? Are you satisfied? Goodbye then.'

I loved this display of monkish jealousy.

In the evening, Lobo wanted to buy a cake as that day also happened to be my birthday. Litang had one too many cake shops. From their big glassy windows, temptation stared at our faces; overgrown cream cakes as tall as humans, smooth peaks of calories, snow-white with giant dragons carved on them, food for some extra-terrestrial species. It was impossible to find a tiny one; people in this town seemed unable to celebrate in small doses. After searching for a long time, we found one shop where two neglected dwarf-cakes sat in a miserable corner. Then we cut the cakes with Longlife's family.

When we woke up the next day, we headed straight for the rooftop because Litang was at its most beautiful under the morning sun. All the peaks surrounding us turned from red to gold and then to white, looking like tiaras worn by the houses of Litang. The dust of the town was yet to rise up and the chanting from the nearby monastery was all that broke the stillness. We followed these holy notes to reach the Litang monastery, commissioned by the Third Dalai Lama in 1580. An endless stream of pilgrims came our way. They were all colourful characters, men and women wearing high boots, cowboy hats and fancy shades. They spun personal prayer wheels as they walked, some carrying them on large staffs. They were in best of moods, greeting us with jubilant 'Tashi deleks'.

The monastery was a formidable complex, its walls encircling an entire mountain. We entered a large hall where an examination was going on. Novice monks stood centre stage one by one and a row of masters seated in the front threw questions on Buddhist theology at them. When the examinee answered, he jumped forward on one leg and clapped with extended hands in one swift motion in the typical style of Tibetan debates. The audience, comprising other candidates, composed an ocean of red robes. They were of all ages, some in their pre-teens, some well into their thirties. When a candidate gave an erroneous response, he bit his tongue, making the audience respond with a roar of chuckles. My presence caused some commotion in the examination process. As I moved around, the people in the audience turned their necks in unison to follow me. When I smiled at them, the youngest ones, who were seated in the back rows, began making faces at me, some acting like monkeys, others like demons, just the way Pema had done in Tagong. Tibetan children seem to consider this as the only appropriate response to me. Of course, I had to rise up to the challenge. I began making faces at them too which made them roll with laughter, ducking behind people sitting in front so that they were not seen by the seniors. This was definitely not appropriate behaviour in a famed monastery. But I was glad to be able to give these children a few seconds of laughter in what was perhaps a life chained to intense discipline.

We walked into the monastery's kitchen where a monk was preparing some kind of gruel in an enormous vat. He could speak a few words of Hindi as he had studied in India.

'*Kaisa hai* (How are you)?' he asked in Hindi. '*Kya kar raha hai* (What are you doing)?'

We were curious about his job.

'This food is for 700 monks,' he said in Mandarin. 'So that makes me the best cook in the world.'

The monk did not offer to let us test his claim. It seemed he just wanted to practise speaking Hindi as he asked again, '*Kya kar raha hai?*'

Then I realised that his Hindi phrases must have been carefully chosen and rehearsed so he could spew them out. Just next to the kitchen was the donation room. I could see two elderly laywomen handing over envelopes and filling up the register for entreaties. From inside this room, the book-keeping monks looked at us quizzically. We just smiled and made a hasty exit.

At the very end of the monastery, we came across the monks' quarters, which were long rows of small rooms on two floors. There was a lone monk cleaning the verandah. He spoke neither Hindi nor Mandarin and so just smiled at us and with a gesture of hand, invited us to walk in. We peeked in through the doors that were open and saw small beds, books and bundles of belongings. I found it remarkable that one could access the private world of the monks so easily. I couldn't help but imagine the situation if reversed, how monks who came to explore our city condominiums uninvited, would be confronted with security guards and CCTV set-ups.

The monastery, however, had closed itself to the world once, leading to its bombing and destruction. After the fall of the Qing dynasty, the 13th Dalai Lama had largely erased the projection of Chinese power over areas inhabited by Tibetans. But soon after his sudden death, squabbles between competing power centres significantly weakened this tentative control of Tibetan aristocracy. At the same time, the Communist wave swept through Mongolia. Tibetans, especially, the monastic cohort, shuddered when they heard the news of the secularization and destruction of monasteries in this region with its deep spiritual and temporal connection to Tibet. So when the Communists eventually 'liberated' Tibet in 1950, there was widespread fear among Tibetans that their age-old way of living was under threat.

Nothing much happened for a few years till groups of comrades began visiting Tibetan areas in 1955-56 to begin 'reforms'. Instead of working through the ground up as was the praxis in other parts of China, in Litang, as in other areas of Amdo and Kham, the reformers decided to start their work from the top, by 'reforming' the monasteries since they were often the largest landowners and were known to deploy corvée labour in Tibet. Once the comrades arrived in Litang, they asked the monastery for details regarding their financial matters and land possessions and also told them to hand over their large stock of old rifles. The monastery refused to cooperate. The stockpile of arms became a major issue as the monastery argued that they were necessary to keep away bandits who the Communists claimed to have eliminated anyway. The monks refused to negotiate and closed the gates of the monastery. Small skirmishes broke out between both sides and the monastery, which perhaps had over 5,000 resident monks, was then besieged by the Chinese army.

When tensions prevailed for more than a month, the Chinese resorted to aerial bombing and destroyed the monastery. Skirmishes continued in Litang well into the following year during which more than 4,000 people were killed. Resistance sprang up in other parts of Kham and Amdo too and guerrilla groups, such as the Chushi Gangdruk, were formed to fight the People's Liberation Army (PLA). The situation escalated further with the Dalai Lama's spectacular escape to India. The CIA made a covert entry to arm the Tibetans and Kham rebels, and formed a large base in northern Nepal to plan offensives. Yet, it was all too late and the Chinese established firm control by 1965. (In a peculiar twist of history, the Magars, descendants of the ancient Kham migrants to Nepal, were the strongest supporters of the Maoist movement in Nepal.)

Yet, even today, despite its seeming prosperity, Litang was an open fuse. From time to time, small-scale trouble erupted, following which foreigners were barred access to this high town with its disproportionate number of CCTVs. In 2007, during the annual Horse Festival, a Kham named Rongyal Adrak seized the microphone from a Chinese official to make an impromptu speech demanding the Dalai

Lama's return. Since then, the Horse Festival, an important milestone in Litang's calendar, has been banned. Small-scale versions of the event were still being organized annually in the town's surroundings.

As we headed out of the monastery, we passed by the main prayer hall that had been severely damaged in 2013 in a massive fire. On that November night, both the Chinese and Tibetans had worked together to put out the flames. Today, the Chinese government was helping in its reconstruction efforts, part of its recent drive to win Tibetan hearts by shunning its earlier practice of subduing the monks and monasteries. Male and female workers, all Tibetans, carried large wooden beams along the construction site and a group of resting workers invited us to have some butter tea with them.

'It's hard work,' said a young worker with the characteristic weather-beaten face. 'But it is for our temple. When it is done, it will be beautiful.'

A new wing had already been built next to the main prayer hall, with an enormous Buddha statue in the centre and countless smaller statues stacked along the walls.

After the monastery, we visited the grounds for a sky burial. While visitors were barred from attending sky burials in Tibet owing to their overenthusiasm in taking photographs, in Tibetan areas outside of Tibet, it was very much possible. The burial ground was located in the outskirts of Litang. It was an open grassland with strange lumps of bushy grass and a lot of garbage. Charred bones and rotting carcasses of rats bejewelled this desolate place. Vultures hovered above. The wind blew strong. A small house stood in the centre. A Tibetan man, dressed in layers of torn jackets, was huffing and puffing inside. He was collecting trash and appeared in great a hurry. When we asked him about the burials, he began a deep-throated song without looking at us:

'Zu tien mei you
Ming tien hai you
Zu tien mei you
Ming tien hai you
Zu tien mei you
Ming tien hai you...'

He drove away in a motorcycle, singing like a maniac. His song, the spookiest I had heard, meant 'There is none today, definitely tomorrow.' Chronicle of a death foretold.

On our way back, Mr Zhao, our taxi driver, became talkative. He had come from the Hunan province and had been living in Litang for four years. His wife worked in a local restaurant.

'I never come to this place,' he said. 'I don't know why you tourists love to see dead bodies getting chopped. What if their spirits turn against you?'

We asked him why he had agreed to bring us over in that case.

'I need money today, as simple as that. But if someone asks me tomorrow, I will refuse. You see I used to be a truck driver. Those days, we could make

100,000 yuan a year driving trucks between Chengdu and Lhasa. Those days the money was good but it was dangerous too. They said that a driver became a man from a boy only once he has driven through the Sichuan–Tibet Highway. But not too long after I became a man, the economy began to slow down. I took to driving a taxi in my hometown but there was no money in it. Xi Da Da (Uncle Xi, the adorable nickname for President Xi Jinping) came out against corruption so no one came out for fun at night. Earlier if A wanted to give B a treat, A would drag along a few friends. Since they will be drinking, most will not drive themselves. Taxi drivers could then make money then. But Xi Da Da put an end to that. So I came here to try my luck. Not much business but less Han people to compete with.'

We asked why money wasn't good in Litang despite the town attracting so many Tibetan pilgrims.

'I would never pick up Tibetans if I could avoid it,' he said. 'When I used to drive in Chengdu, the taxi company instructed us to never pick up Tibetans. But here, I have little choice.'

'Why? What do you have against Tibetans?' asked Lobo.

'Bad people! They are very bad people. They will rush you: hey, why are you so slow? I'm in a rush! They will make you speed through red lights. Once they reach, they never pay. Another time the guy had a fruit knife. I couldn't argue nor call the police. No use calling the police anyway. It would have been too late.'

Zhao went on, 'Once a Tibetan took my cab. He complained that it was very hard for Tibetans to get cabs. I told him, "Yes, I understand it's hard for you to get cabs. But have you thought about how hard it is for us to get paid by people like you? Who do we complain to?" These people look poor but actually they are not. Many are rich or live a pretty decent life. Once a Tibetan guy threw a stack of cash on my dashboard saying, "I have money! But it's mine! Why should I give it to you?" They always behave badly. Their women are still okay, but the men are really bad. They are lazy. They want easy money. Actually the ones from Lhasa are better, maybe it's because it's a big city.'

We asked Zhao about the relationship between Hans and Tibetans in Litang. He put his hand up and waved angrily to signal a 'No'.

There was another Zhao who was known across Kham as 'Zhao, the Butcher'. Appointed by the Qing emperor to subdue Tibetan violence against Chinese officials in Kham (in response to the accommodation of French Catholic missionaries by the Chinese in Kham), Zhao Erfeng ran a violent campaign from 1905 to 1911 from his base in Litang. He targeted the monks in particular. At his peak, Zhao extended his domain all the way to Lhasa, which forced the 13th Dalai Lama to flee to India. However, after the Republican revolution of 1911 that overthrew Puyi, the child emperor, Zhao was implicated by Republican forces and then beheaded in Chengdu. Till today, the memory of 'Zhao, the Butcher' remains strong in the Tibetan community.

Back in town, we visited the house where the Seventh Dalai Lama had been born. It was marked with a small metal board titled 'Renkang House'. Seven coconut-like balls hung on its doorway. The place was surprisingly lonely. Inside, we visited the cowshed where the Seventh's mother had given birth, a site heavily draped with colourful scarves. Once we came out, Zhao was still there, hoping to get more passengers. When we told him that no one else was inside, he gave us an impromptu description of the place even after we told him that we didn't need his taxi service any more.

'Did you see the cowshed?' he asked. 'Did you see the Dalai Lama's baby footprints there? You know why he was born there of all places, in a cowshed? Because Tibetans believed that childbirth is dirty and brings evil. So they always took the mother outside the main house, in places like a cowshed. That's what the tourists tell me.'

'The Seventh was the best,' Zhao went on. 'These Tibetans say the Fifth was the greatest but he was a politician. And the Sixth was a drunkard. So I say the Seventh was the best. You know he started to speak as soon as he was born. Amazing, right? That's what the tourists tell me.'

Born in 1708, the Seventh was the most well-known son of Litang but it was the Sixth who gave Litang its fame, all because of those four lines of poetry he had composed. The Sixth was born in 1683 in Tawang, not too far from where I was born, the small town of Lumding in Assam. Initially, his identity was kept secret as the Desi (Regent) of Tibet had skilfully managed to hide the news of the death of the great Fifth for 15 years to avoid any turbulence. Right from the start, the Sixth showed no inclination for lama life. As he grew into a teenager, he became infamous for enjoying a good life, often going out with his friends to drink chang (Tibetan beer) and spend long nights with the women of Lhasa. According to one legend, every girl the Sixth visited would then paint the door of her house yellow and it was not long before Lhasa ran out of this colour. In his short life, he composed around 50 to 60 poems. These poems, celebrating love and the good things in life with an occasional burst of self-righteousness, were still read widely, more so in China than in Tibet, where the Sixth remained well loved. One of his poems went:[8]

People gossip about me
I am sorry for what I have done
I have taken three steps
And landed myself in the tavern of my mistress…

Some of his defenders argued that these poems were far from erotic and were in fact tantric codes. But the Desi reprimanded him often for not changing his ways and even tried to get him killed once.

Tibet soon entered a turbulent phase as Lazhang Khan, a pious yet violent Mongol, took control of Lhasa. He killed the Desi and replaced the Sixth with his own candidate. The Sixth knew that his time was limited and during his forced transfer to Beijing, wrote those immortal lines about Litang. Soon after, in 1706, he disappeared mysteriously. Although historians agree that he was killed on Lazhang's orders, some

Tibetans believe that he escaped to Mongolia where he went on to live anonymously for another 40 years.

But the Sixth would yet have his revenge, through his poem. Aware of those lines, Tibetans looked for signs in Litang and a monk in Litang's monastery got the chief oracle to identify the boy from Renkang House. To protect the new Seventh from Lhazang, the young boy was raised and groomed secretly in the monastery to be the next Dalai Lama. Tibetans— those who knew—anxiously waited for the time when the Seventh could be brought to where he belonged rightfully, which was the Potala Palace, the fortress in Lhasa where the Dalai Lamas would spend winter. With their support, the Dzungar Mongols invaded Tibet in 1717 and fired the impostor Sixth amid many street celebrations in Lhasa. Lhazang himself was cut to pieces as he tried to flee. But the Dzungars, too, were no better as they took to widespread looting, raping and behaving like bandits. In 1720, with the help of the Chinese emperor, an exiled Tibetan aristocrat called Polhanas drove the Dzungars out and a year later, the Seventh finally came to Lhasa to claim his title. The Seventh wrote poetry too. Laced with religiosity and righteousness, his work couldn't be farther from that of the Sixth.

Soon enough, the Seventh and Polhanas were caught in a fresh game of politicking and the Seventh was sent back to Litang. Polhanas succeeded him as the ruler of Tibet but the relationship between Potala and Beijing turned sour gradually. One fine day in Lhasa, Polhanas was tricked and killed by the representatives of the Qing emperor. The Tibetans revolted violently but order was forced on to Tibet by an invading Qing army. The emperor ordered the formation of a local council of ministers to run Tibet's daily affairs, and sent two ambans or monitors to Lhasa. To pacify the Tibetans, the Qing emperor brought back the Seventh to Lhasa, after an exile of 22 years. He was crowned the 'temporal head' of Tibet with few actual powers and it was during the time of the Seventh that Tibet became a sort of protectorate of China. Though the real control exercised by the ambans peaked and troughed at different times in history, the world—at least the governments of its nation states—bought the Chinese argument of Tibet being a part of China because of its reference to that arrangement that was forced on the Seventh Dalai Lama by the then Chinese emperor.

We left Litang soon. On the route, I thought of one of the Sixth's poems:[9]

To say farewell
Is to be sad
Be not sad, my love
For after every parting
Comes another meeting.

Eight

The 'Other' Shangri-La

Shangri-La stands for confusion. There could be none, one, two, seven or thousands of Shangri-Las. Shangri-La was an invention, an imaginary place named by James Hilton in his bestselling novel titled *Lost Horizon*. Hilton drew his inspiration from descriptions of the Tibetan borderlands in Sichuan and Yunnan by other travellers. But who were these travellers? That remains a mystery. They could have been French travellers from the mid-nineteenth century, or Joseph Rock, an explorer from the National Geographic, who trekked through these areas in the early twentieth century. Locating Shangri-La was, therefore, left to speculation. Yet, finding it was a serious job. The stakes were high as whichever place proved to be the real Shangri-La could win a massive bounty in the context of the boom in domestic tourism in China.

The county of Zhongdian in Yunnan made the first move. In 2001, it renamed itself as Shangri-La. Zhongdian cashed in big as millions of Chinese tourists flocked to the town after this renaming. Not to be left behind, the county of Riwa, where we were headed to, took the gamble and renamed itself Shangri-La the year after. Riwa's claim was not taken too seriously. Yet, the growing reputation of the fall colours of the nearby Yading Reserve drew hordes of domestic tourists to this Shangri-La wannabe every year. Consequently, Riwa and Yading were now looking like any other tourism megaplex in China with its tense each-one-for-himself crowds, massive queues, Technicolor neon signages, expensive roundtable restaurants, caterpillar mushroom pharmacies and the obligatory Karaoke (KTV) parlours , so popular in East and Southeast Asia—as far from the idea of Shangri-La as it was possible. Or did all this make Riwa as close to it as was possible?

Shangri-La was also an idea, a land of happy people who lived long lives—contented, harmonious, emancipated, healthy, strong, youthful and free from all ailments. But central to this idea of Shangri-La was the requirement of remoteness. That posed a counternarrative to all the technological and intellectual achievements of humanity by suggesting their irrelevance and misguidedness when it came to founding a utopia. Wasn't it the Shangri-La disconnected from modern drugs, political parties and smartphones that had achieved all that we sought to attain?

We shared the van from Litang to Riwa with a small group of Chinese tourists. I always enjoyed travelling with Chinese groups because they provided an endless streaming of wisecracks, a good percentage of which were indeed very funny. This van was no different. Our co-passengers were all female, coming from Chengdu. They were constantly harassing the Tibetan driver. The girls were perhaps in their early 30s and the driver was probably of the same age. With his thin face, hooked nose and big eyes, our driver, unlike other Tibetan men we had met before, had a rather 'Come, harass me' feel about him. But he knew how to hold his own fort.

'Oh, why you don't give us a discount?' said one girl. 'You were already the luckiest driver in the world with so many girls in your car. Now you have a man too. What more do you want?'

'Oh no, I can't,' said the driver. 'It is a fixed price. If I give you a discount, the other drivers will punish me in the old Tibetan way, by squeezing my head with a band till the eyeballs pop out.'

The driver had a point. Tibetan culture, contrary to its reputation for its emphasis on peace and non-violence, practised this unusual form of punishment for high treason. A metal band would be placed just above the victim's eyes and the band tightened gradually till the pressure forced the eyeballs to pop out of their sockets. One of the most remarkable victims of this form of justice was Lungshar, one of Tibet's great reformers or great traitors, depending on who wrote about him. Lungshar had been sent to Britain by the 13th Dalai Lama as part of a small group to get educated the Western way. Once the group returned, Lungshar became a modernizer running against a stopwatch. He rose up the ranks fast to become one of the top three bureaucrats in Tibet. But when the 13th Dalai Lama died, the resulting power vacuum led to a lot of scheming and counterscheming in which Lungshar excelled initially before being completely outmanoeuvred. He was charged for colluding with the Communists to organize a coup. The blinding was carried out in 1936 and he died a year later. Some Tibetans still ponder if Tibet's history would have taken an entirely different track if Lungshar had succeeded in bringing about a modern state that might have stood up to the People's Liberation Army.

We were passing through Konkaling, an area that was once infamous for its hostility to outsiders. Up until recently, any Chinese person who dared to enter these badlands would be slaughtered as soon as he was spotted. The same greeting was offered to Tibetans who came from other parts. But these days, Chinese tourists travelled through these roads in thousands to photograph the numerous lakes that were leftovers from an ancient glacial cap (some historians believe that 2,000 years ago, the expansion of these glaciers destroyed a magnificent Kham civilization and forced many Khams to migrate to Nepal).

'It is not fair,' said our fellow passenger, a little coldly, 'We town people come to your villages to spend money. But you village people never come to our towns to spend and develop our economy. If you can't give us a discount, at least give us some caterpillar mushrooms.'

'I can,' said the driver. 'But then you will be delayed very badly. The mushroom season comes after six months. Do you want me to stop and wait till then?'

The girl got distracted by yaks grazing in the distance.

'I know why Chinese cooking tastes different from your Tibetan cooking,' said the girl. 'Because you use yak dung while we use gas.'

Suddenly, our motormouth co-passenger screamed, 'Hey, have you seen a yeren (yeti)? Isn't this supposed to be the land of the yeti?'

The driver said, 'Yes, of course.'

'Show us one, we will give you 5 yuan more.'

'No way,' retorted the driver. 'You Han people will then take away its skin.'

The only temple in the world dedicated to the yeti was also located in Sichuan, in the Jiulong county, not too far from Kangding. It was also in Sichuan that the latest yeti was caught. That happened as recently as 2010 though the yeti looked rather like a balding puppy.[10]

I had been mesmerized by yetis as a child. They

featured aplenty in cheap Bengali novellas, reading which I assumed yetis to be giant avuncular creatures, getting annoyed by the unjust definition in the dictionary of the yeti as 'the abominable snowman'. I imagined that yetis hid in our midst by assuming human forms, revealing their true white, hairy and huge selves only when no one was looking. I devised a simple test to spill the beans on yetis posing as humans by the size of the slippers of people I suspected of actually being yetis. After all, why would a yeti bother buying two sets of slippers, a small size for the human form and a large one for his real identity? Friends of our parents or relatives would always be delighted when immediately after we exchanged pleasantries, I would offer to keep their sandals at a proper place. What a well-mannered child, these unsuspecting elders would have imagined. Those were the days of bad fashion and there were enough people wearing oversized slippers. So I lived in a world where a good third of the humans I knew were actually yetis. I would spy on them, looking for more signs. But they would always use the eyes at the back of their heads to figure me out and stay discreet. As I grew up, I lost interest in them. But when we had first arrived at Chengdu and visited Lobo's friend, I spotted a pair of enormous slippers at her house, perhaps three times the size of her feet. It had fluffy pink hair coming out of everywhere, even from its soles. She explained that it was a Japanese invention to keep mopping the house as one walked around. Right, Yeti Girl!

Just before Daocheng was a valley of red grasslands. Thousands of Chinese tourists were already there in their colourful jackets. The girls also got down to take some photographs.

'Wait for us for half an hour,' one of the girls told the driver. 'Don't you dare leave without us! I want to photograph the scenery.'

But soon, they realized that it was difficult to frame nature without including humanity. As they came back to the car within two minutes, they grumbled, 'Look at all these people. In China, it is now impossible to visit any good attraction in peace.'

The driver chuckled, 'If you all hadn't come, there would be a little more peace. And I wouldn't have gotten a headache from talking to you.'

The sun was setting by the time we arrived in Riwa. There were too many cars, buses and vans, all stuck in an unresolvable traffic jam. This was the peak week for tourists as Yading turned up in its best colours during this late autumn period. We looked around for a place to spend the night. But everyone else had the same idea. The entire town seemed to have nothing other than hotels; yet, the demand was overwhelming and all hotels were charging exorbitant rates. People with backpacks crisscrossed the narrow road, entering a place and then coming out within 30 seconds to look for another. An elderly Han woman approached us and offered to take us to a cheaper place. She took us through some narrow alleys to a private apartment masquerading as a hotel (without a licence) and asked for 450 yuan. As we walked away, the lady screamed at us, 'How can you expect any rates cheaper than this? This is Shangri-La.'

Once the rush for rooms calmed down and the hotels realized that they would still be left with some inventory, prices fell in big jumps and we secured a characterless room next to the hotel laundry for only 100 yuan. Of course, our hotel was named Shangri-La, one of the four that we had come across in Riwa, none of them having anything to do with the Hong Kong chain. Overjoyed at the success of our own cunning, we decided to have a hearty meal in a Shandong dumpling restaurant just a few steps away. As we walked in, all the other customers turned to talk to us and asked us in a chorus, 'How much did you pay for your hotel?'

We told them the rack rate to protect our hotel's receptionist from any harassment. They shrugged collectively and one of them said, 'They are all robbers here. And this is only the other Shangri-La. But we shouldn't complain. Only the gods are supposed to be able to afford room rents in heaven.'

We spent the whole night sleeplessly, listening to the drilling and scratching of cement as the excavators cut off the hills, bite by bite, rock by rock, to create more livable spaces in the other Shangri-La.

We left for Yading at sunrise the next day. Just as we had expected, the whole trip to Yading was now managed in a very Chinese way, with merciless ticket prices, ticket counters far from the actual site to allow a monopoly transport provider to charge high prices for dropping tourists, huge crowds and a general scramble. Yet, all this came with a great infrastructure, without which travelling to this remote wilderness would have been nearly impossible. The monopoly on transport also allowed better management of the nature reserve. So despite the initial jostling around for tickets, everything ran relatively smoothly for us.

There were little signs of Yading's glory till the drop-off point for the park bus. But from there onwards, our spirits were taken to a high as we took the see-through metal staircase that climbed over a gentle waterfall shaded by trees celebrating in a bright abundance of yellow and red. Soon, a vast landscape opened up to us and our already gaping mouths stretched beyond their biological limits as we faced Mount Jambeyang in brilliant white, framed on the sides by lush green hills, a dazzling blue sky as the roof, and a vast orange grassland as the floor. It was nature as we had known only in cheap calendars.

We didn't mind the thousands of other tourists around us, eagerly snapping selfies and wefies. The beauty here at Chonggu Pasture was too vast and it absorbed us all. On the other hand, I felt a strange bonding with all these strangers who were now sharing the same appreciation that I felt for this splendour. The tension at the ticketing counters was a distant memory as everyone was smiling, not just among their kith and kin but also when their eyes crossed with a stranger's. What made us humans love snowy mountains, clear streams, crisp mountain air and blue skies? Wasn't it in our inherent interest to destroy them all with civilization? Or had nature subtly carved in a defence mechanism for itself in our genes, a love of pristine nature and a desire to conserve it as a balance to our instincts as exploitative raiders?

We moved around leisurely, our eyes fixed on the peaks. We were trying to soak it all in, breathing deep as if that would print Yading permanently as wallpaper memories. One good hour later, we finally decided to move on. Fifteen minutes of climbing took us to Chonggu Gompa, also known as the 'Bandit Monastery'. Joseph Rock had described this place as an abode of notorious criminals who despite being career-monks, terrorized neighbouring villages and passing caravans by murdering and robbing people. The monastery gave little hints of this boisterous past. Chubby monks were sunning themselves in the yard and the only horror in the monastery was that of a miserable monkey chained to a log. It kept jumping up and down desperately to escape as the monks watched it with bored eyes, seemingly oblivious to their own belief that Tibetans originated from monkeys, a creation myth surprisingly close to Darwinian brilliance (some also believe that Tibetans originated from the Kauravas, the defeated brothers in the epic, the Mahabharata).

An elderly group of Chinese tourists tried to engage the bored monks by asking about the monastery. One of the monks said, 'This monastery is very important. People have seen miracles here. Sometimes, the face of Manjushri, the bodhisattva of great wisdom, suddenly appears in these mountains.'

As we followed this group of Chinese tourists out of the monastery, we heard one of the women from the group whisper, 'These monks look scary. This monastery too. I think there are some strange spirits in such places. I never pray at their temples. There was once when I prayed at a Tibetan monastery and the next day I got severe diarrhoea.'

Another 45 minutes of climbing though colourful foliage took us to a small rocky valley where Chinese tourists had written messages with stones. Most of these messages talked about love stories. Five minutes later we came across a viewing platform from where Mount Chenresig was visible for the first time. A tanned and bearded Tibetan monk was putting up quite a show there by prostrating himself, facing the mountain. Several tourists were photographing him. From time to time, he was requested to pose for a wefie to which he always obliged. Some tourists gave him small notes for this. After we passed by him, we arrived at the Pearl Lake, having reached an elevation of 4,140 m. The lake reflected the peak of Mount Chenresig perfectly. We jostled with the tourists to find the best spot for photography. In China, in the previous year, the most popular way to pose for pictures was to look like a turning airplane, arms outstretched like wings fitted to a tilted body. All at once, Chinese people from Harbin, the capital of Heilongjiang, China's northernmost province, to Golmud, the third largest city in the Tibetan Plateau, posed the same way. But this year's pose was to stand straight and raise one hand high above the head, proudly holding a mobile phone.

The crowd had thickened considerably by the time we went back to the first viewpoint. It was already past noon and many were munching on their takeaway lunches, bananas and packed sausages for most. Sensing the opportunity, stray goats and squirrels begged for food while birds retained their pride as they snatched tidbits thrown to them and flew away, pretending they were unnoticed. A mother and child duo of goats walked up to me and leaned on me by standing on their hind legs and placing their front legs on my waist, demanding the precious bread that I had for my vegetarian lunch. They climbed down only when I sacrificed the entire lot of bread to them. A group of tourists surrounded me to snap photographs of these shameless reincarnations of Konkaling bandits.

We reached Lurong Pasture (4,180 metre) after walking 6 km. It was an open area of orange grasslands, pockmarked with pockets of blue ponds. Clouds had rolled into Yading by then, ricocheting from one peak to another. In one transient moment of clarity, however, we could see all the three peaks surrounding Lurong Pasture for the first time: Mount Chenresig named after the bodhisattva of compassion, Mount Chanadorje or the bodhisattva of power, holder of the thunderbolt, and Mount Jambeyang or Manjushri, the bodhisattva of wisdom. Both Jambeyang and Chanadorje were 5,958 metre high, while Chenresig superseded them by another 74 metre. Joseph Rock had talked about these mountains, Jambeyang in particular, as the most beautiful mountains in the world. Even though Rock was prone to the overuse of orgasmic prose, a certificate of excellence from a man who must have seen several mountains stood as a solid testimonial. Indeed, Jambeyang was a sharp pointed beauty, looking like a magician's wand hidden behind a white handkerchief. As I was looking at it, I scratched my beard and I recalled a haiku by Matsuo

Basho, the Japanese Zen poet (1644–94):

Sight of that mountain
makes me forget
I'm getting old…

We were standing at Mount Jambeyang's foot, from where it rose up straight. Like all mountains appeared to non-mountaineers, it seemed to be an easy climb, just half an hour of effort and we could be balancing ourselves at its knife-edged peak. Though they were much shorter than the basketball star peaks of the Himalayas, none of the three mountains had ever been climbed. Their invincibility was partly because Tibetans considered it sacrilegious for anyone to climb atop these holy peaks. Yet, clandestine attacks had been made from time to time, all known to be failures.

Tibetans came from far to perform a kora or circumambulation of these three holy mountains. In his book, *Shangri-La: A Practical Guide to the Himalayan Dream,* Michael Buckley wrote that 15 koras around these three Konkaling mountains were equal to a hundred million utterings of the Tibetan mantra *Om Mani Padme Hum.*

A gruff man approached us at Lurong. He hugged me abruptly, held my face firmly in his yeti-hands, and almost planted a kiss. 'Your beard is so nice,' he said with a boisterous laugh. 'Please give it to me. Women here love such beards and seeing one like yours will be full of admiration: let me kiss you, let me please.'

Our newest friend went by the name of Namgyal. 'I

am a cleaner in the park,' he said. 'I live over there.' He pointed to the handful of Tibetan huts located across the stream that ran around Lurong Pasture.

'My family used to be nomads,' Namgyal said. 'We come here for the tourist season to rent horses. Earlier, the only way for people to visit Yading was to hire horses, porters and guides from us. We could charge a lot. But then they built the roads and got these electric carts. Still, nomads here can rent horses to take people to the lakes, on shorter trips.'

We asked Namgyal how many horses he owned.

'I have no horses,' he said. 'My brother has three. But that doesn't mean anything to me. People keep complaining about the roads, but they like to complain. They can still rent horses at very high prices and nowadays there are so many more tourists. I don't have a horse, so this is the only way I can live. The more tourists come to Yading, the more I have to clean. But for people like my brother, more tourists mean more money. Still, they like to complain.'

'We Tibetans don't understand business like you Chinese do,' he said. 'All these tourists started coming only about three years ago. And then we saw more and more Chinese people settling down in Yading and Riwa. Most of them are from Fujian, the province on the southeast coast of China, and I think they speak Hokkien. They came and then signed long-term rental contracts with us for our houses. They paid Tibetans 100,000 yuan a year. They said they will pay this for ten years. We Tibetans were very happy to sign. Then these people renovated the houses and shops and within a year rented them out to other Han businessmen at three times the price. My brother leased out his house and I became very angry but what can he do? He has signed a contract. It is not the Fujian guy's fault. Why does he complain then? This is how we are, we don't know how to do business, especially the older generation. Like we saw these tourists come here earlier with a lot of batteries and films. It just didn't strike us Tibetans that we could sell these things to them here. We only realized after we saw Han stores in Riwa full of batteries and films. And then we complain.'

Namgyal's words confused me. While I found his comparison of Tibetan and Han business instincts rather plausible, I was not sure what inspired him to want to buy my beard.

We returned to Riwa and spent the evening at our favourite Shandong dumpling restaurant again. The owner offered me a special drink from Shandong that he promised was a hundred times stronger than any 'Western' alcohol. Chinese have this penchant for comparing everything with 'Western' counterparts— medicine, food, lifestyle, values, ideology. When I finished the small glass without blacking out, the avuncular man was delighted.

'You are the big boss,' he said. 'This man is the big boss.'

Before going back to our hotel, we scanned the supermarket for the next day's meal on the mountains.

The place was a treasure trove of processed food, Angela's chemical junkyard, including preserved pig ears, yak entrails and duck colon, the list of preservatives on their labels running way longer than the name of the main ingredient. Even the bread smelled strongly of burning tyres. We bought a pile of bananas, the food that seemed to have the smallest concentration of petrochemicals. I hid the bananas deep inside my backpack and plotted a mental map of where I could eat them the next day, safe from the greedy goats.

The next day, we arrived rather early at the ticket counters. Our ticket was valid for three entries but we still had to get them endorsed, a process put in place to make sure that no single-day trippers were passing on their tickets to newcomers for discounted prices. It was still dark but there was a massive queue. An elderly tourist explained, 'Today is the last day of the official tourist season. And we Chinese love to follow everything official.'

When it was our turn, the hassled-looking ticketing lady asked us for proof of our visit the previous day. When we told her that we had forgotten to get our tickets stamped the day before, she asked us to show pictures of Yading from then. We showed her our mobile. She scanned through a few and then asked us,

'These are all pictures of mountains and lakes. You could have downloaded them from the internet, so show me your own selfies against Yading scenery.'

Now, when it came to taking selfies, we were a couple

who ranked very low among global couples. And even though I remembered taking some solo shots of Lobo in front of Jambeyang, I had not allowed any photographs of myself because of my firm conviction that my presence in the frame would severely degrade the images of this magnificent landscape. So after I showed Lobo's picture to the ticketing lady, I panicked as I searched my phone desperately for a picture, but couldn't find one. What could I do? She was looking at me sternly. Lobo pushed me aside and showed her phone to the lady and both nodded at each other with a smile.

She said, 'Good, you can go in now. Why didn't you tell me this before?'

What was it? What had happened? How could this lady even know how to smile? Bewildered, I asked Lobo what magic lay in her phone. After much nagging, she showed me her phone. She had secretly filmed Namgyal trying to kiss me the previous day. I wanted to go back, running. I had to explain—I was not what the lady was thinking. Lobo was my wife, I had to tell that to her. Why did Lobo have to do this? I turned back and was blocked immediately by the fenced queue that stretched all the way to Beijing.

Once we reached Chonggu Pasture, we took an electric cart straight to Lurong. Our plan was to walk all the way from Lurong to Milk Lake and Five Colour Lake, through a route that formed part of the kora, a challenging high-altitude trek.

It had snowed all night at Yading. The landscape

had transformed overnight. All the colours were gone as everything was blanketed by white and grey, a black and white photograph of yesterday. The clouds cleared soon, the breeze came to a halt, and the grassland of Lurong became a wetland with several placid pools that gave the holy peaks of Yading a perfect excuse to admire their own appearance in the clear reflections that formed in these transient waterbodies. The tourists, ecstatic from this magical moment, scrambled to take pictures. It was forbidden to walk on the grasslands but this mass delight was impossible to control. Some haphazardly fixed their tripods on the uneven land; others ran clumsily through puddles to secure the best spot. Alas, the tourists were getting reflected too and all images showed the glorious mountains and their reflections partitioned by a thin layer of huddled bodies in colourful winter jackets.

Most tourists did not go any further from Lurong. Yet there were more than 500 tourists who joined us for the trek up to the Milk Lake, some renting horses from the nomads. The route began as a gentle trail and then began to climb continuously. The snowmelt was coming down the same route and all of us stumbled through a muddy, slippery mess. After an hour of walking, we climbed above the tree line. From there onwards, it was a steep rocky scramble. Elderly tourists, who had not adjusted to the altitude before, gave up, asking their younger companions to fetch them on their way back. Some, who had brought along big oxygen pillows, sucked on them like voracious newborns. Nomads teased the strugglers to take up their services or perish. Along with their horses, these cheeky businessmen had been a constant annoyance for trekkers. They wanted to climb fast and make as much money as they could on the last day of the season, whistling and shouting angrily at trekkers to give way in that narrow and slippery path.

Having spent a few weeks at such a high altitude, we were at the top of the pack to reach the Milk Lake. Despite my struggle at Tagong, I felt in perfect condition in Yading. All the preparatory exercises I had done at the sea-level city of Singapore were finally bearing fruit. But when I suggested to Lobo that we do a kora of the Milk Lake (elevation: 4,600 metre), she refused.

'This is already the highest I have been in my life,' she said. 'You go ahead while I catch some breath and prepare for the next climb.'

To show off, I ran for my kora.

I found myself all alone at the other end of the small lake. I sat down to look at the reflections of a series of snowy peaks, this time without the zipperlike layer of colourful tourists. Could I just become a permanent fixture there, like a mani stone? Mani stones have the Tibetan Buddhism mantra *Om Mani Padme Hum* inscribed on them and they are placed on roads or along rivers as offerings to spirits.

I had a peculiar problem with experiencing nature. While places of outstanding natural beauty such as Yading or the Kelimutu Lakes in Indonesia got me genuinely exhilarated, that feeling would disappear soon. Within a week of visiting such a place, I would struggle to flashback the pictures in my mind. On the other hand, what I would remember most from any trip would be the interactions with mankind, small favours from strangers, and interesting quips, or even a minor insult. I would possibly forget everything about Yading too and remember only the short course on Tibetan microeconomics given by Namgyal, the beard-loving cleaner. Perhaps, my attitude towards conservation had also been shaped from such a mindset. I used to care little for the deluge of plastic bags and the destruction of forests. This was until I saw an anthropomorphic image, that of an orangutan mother and child desperately clinging to each other after being rescued from a forest set on fire by loggers in Indonesia. The agonized expressions of the two animals who had also been stoned by nearby villagers had moved me enough to think about how our immediate and remote actions affect these unsuspecting creatures. My turn to vegetarianism had also been largely inspired by anthropomorphic similes that attributed intelligence and pain-sensitivity to animals. Sitting there at the Milk Lake, I tried to imagine those peaks ravaged by climate change, denuded of snow, the lake as a dry pit. Would I ever come back? Probably not. Did I even care then? How could helpless Yading appeal to me with a human face? It tried. As I went back to Lobo, she pointed towards Jambeyang. Everyone was photographing it excitedly. The shadows and depressions on the snow face just beneath its peak had created a recognizable pattern, a human head with eyes, nose and lips.

Lobo said, 'These tourists are saying that's the face of Manjushri.'

From the Milk Lake, we trekked up for another 20 minutes to reach the highest point of our trip. At 4,700 metre, this was also the maximum altitude Lobo had been to yet. From there, the Five Colour Lake was just a 10-minute walk downhill but since it didn't appear that impressive, we decided to walk back. The weather at Yading, which has its own micro-climate, changed frequently with heavy snowfall and bright sunshine swapping places intermittently.

It was four in the evening, two hours before the park's closing time, when we reached Chonggu Pasture. There was a massive queue for the bus back to Riwa. Thousands of people were packed inside a fenced area that led to the loading points. We joined in and were soon swallowed by humanity. Backpacks and fluffy jackets built up a kaleidoscopic ocean with heads floating on top. Initially, everyone was being reasonably civil. Soon, there was some gentle pushing and shoving. Occasional screams emanated from the front of the queue.

'Why do you all keep pushing?' someone said to the person standing behind him. 'If the queue in the front is not moving, what's the use of using force?'

'No, no,' the man behind him said in a gentle voice, 'It is not my fault. It is the way pressure transmits in a funnel. You see, we are now all arranged like a funnel.' He then proceeded to give a long scientific explanation that impressed everyone around him.

Branches and twigs arching over our path threatened to poke us in the eyes and nostrils. Some people took the initiative to break these wayward branches from the fabled trees of Yading. In the jostle, our neighbours changed constantly. An hour passed but we moved forward less than 50 m. Suddenly, I realized that we were surrounded by elderly people. All the young had melted and squeezed out through the fissures. One white-haired man next to me sighed,

'Look at what they put in the brochures—the Land of the Wild and the Free. Those people are probably just typing such junk from a small office in Shanghai. I am not even free to scratch my nose now.'

A Tibetan woman, who had been selling trinkets to tourists, tried to break the queue as she ran to a bus from outside the fenced area. A guard in army camouflage followed her and pulled her out from the bus, scolding her heavily. Everyone turned their necks to see what was happening. I couldn't see properly but smelled a scandal, a burning proof of Han oppression. The man next to me whispered to his wife, 'The soldier is not Han. He is Tibetan.'

After two hours, we boarded a bus with the last group of travellers. While we descended, a huge rainbow formed over the mountains. As our bus changed directions while tracing the winding road, the passengers scurried from one side to another to catch a glimpse.

'So lucky, we are so lucky,' said one old lady.

'Buddha rewarded us for being the last group,' said another.

'Miracle, it's a miracle,' said another, marvelling at what was probably a frequent natural occurrence at Yading.

Once we reached Riwa, there was a traffic jam just outside the bus station caused by all the cars ferrying tourists back to their hotels in Riwa. We wanted to leave the city and spend the night at Daocheng instead. Travel writers who wrote about Shangri-La invariably repeated the cliché that it wasn't a physical place but just a state of mind. I was, however, leaving Shangri-La, the place, in a confused state of mind. The mountains and valleys definitely surpassed expectations. But with its abundance of selfie-sticks, Shangri-La had also appeared like a much detested photography studio in my hometown, with cheap wallpaper. Stuck for two hours at Riwa's massive traffic choke, I eventually realized that Shangri-La was merely the world beyond the jam.

Nine

Highland Cool Chic

Once the jam relaxed, Drolma, our Tibetan driver, drove like an erstwhile F1 champion on a losing streak with one last chance for redemption. We blazed through the dark winding road, skidding at the turns, overtaking any lesser being that came our way. But he stopped all of a sudden. He had spotted a group of elderly Han tourists who were trying to flag him down. Their car had broken down on this lonely road and they were looking for help desperately. Drolma tinkered with the van unsuccessfully. Then he called some repairmen he knew. It was a long conversation that seemed to not just dwell on the current problem on hand, but also sought to solve the Israel–Palestine conflict. We and the other passengers in our car, a group of Chinese students, were getting impatient. I was both charmed by this Tibetan's attempt to help the Chinese and distressed thinking about having to search for hotels rather late in a cold highland town. After 30 minutes of waiting, we forced Drolma to leave the Chinese oldies in the hands of Chenresig.

'No problem,' he said with a smile. 'My friend is on his way and will be reaching soon to fix it. I was on the phone to make sure he didn't turn back.'

We reached Daocheng around 10 at night. The temperature was well below freezing. Everyone except us had a hotel booking and Drolma told us that most hotels would already be full. He dropped us at a place with the highest concentration of cheap hotels. Indeed, all the rooms were booked and if any vacant room was available, it was priced well beyond our budget. Lobo and I walked around in the lonely night from place to place, looking for a place to sleep. After much searching, we found a hotel run by a young Han woman. She said, 'We don't have any rooms but walk three blocks and you will find a big hotel which has a green laser light on its top. Next to it is a brick house with no lights. It is a hotel run by my friend. It's new so they don't have any banner. You will definitely find rooms there.'

We followed the laser beam and reached this spooky place. Two Han man opened the door. They showed us a room with the right price and a cool vibe, deliberately unfinished walls, a flower vase and log-framed windows. The young men were very friendly, talking in super-humble voices. And then there was a power outage.

'Sorry, sorry, so sorry,' said Li, apparently the boss. 'We are new to this business and I didn't have enough capital to buy a generator. If you want, I can light a fire for you downstairs. I just feel so sorry. We can get some hot water and tea for you.'

We took up his offer and the four of us sat down in the dark next to a wooden fire. We talked about our respective lives. I was particularly interested to know what their age was for they looked like teenagers.

'I am 28, while my friend here is 17. He is a baby boy,' Li giggled. Fan Cheng, the baby boy, hid his face in shame.

'I come from Chongqing in southwest China while Fan is from Sichuan,' Li said. 'I used to be a dancer, ballet and classical. As part of my dance troupe, I travelled all around China. When I came here I sensed an opportunity and leased this building. I met Fan at a restaurant here. He was working there at that time. We decided to team up. We are only one month into operations. Our hotel is still not that popular but I hope it's just a matter of time. So many other hotels here began that way and are doing great now. The number of Chinese tourists keeps increasing every year and there are foreigners too who even come during winter to do scientific studies. In winter, there are also adventurers who come for the thrill of it. We just need to work hard. For example, we initially thought of hiring cleaners but we just do everything ourselves now.'

I was rather amused to think of hotel owners

cleaning so many toilet bowls every day.

Li said that the famed Chinese business spirits were rubbing onto Tibetans too. 'There are many Tibetan guest houses also. Many of them are unlicensed but they get support from the Tibetan drivers who drop off customers only at their place.'

Li asked us how we found out about his place and when we mentioned the young woman, his eyes brightened up.

'Oh yes,' he said. 'She is such a nice person.'

I asked if Li missed home.

'I am more worried that my family doesn't miss me. It is indeed lonely over here but sometimes we spend time with other young people like us, like the lady you met before.'

Li blushed as he mentioned her. There were clearly some hints of a love story at work.

The next morning, Daocheng's sky was as blue as the deep sea. Tibetan songs, especially the ones popular in China, often extol the blue sky, perhaps rather too frequently. Only a handful of musicals acts, such as Vajara, the pioneering Tibetan rock and roll band, have dared to deviate from such time-tested standards.[11]

Daocheng had a certain 'Western chic' about it. Hotel lobbies felt cosy with big pedigree dogs and grumpy-eyed Japanese cats lying over welcome mats. At one place, there was a signage for breakfast: 'Headbanger Coffee'. Smooth jazz whiffed out from another window. Perhaps the reason why Daocheng had the vibe of places like Chiang Mai or Bali was because most of the tourists who stayed over in Daocheng were college students or young professionals. They were mostly from Sichuan, their home province. The town still had an abundance of Chinglish signages, such as Ya Lu Underwear Monopoly, Too Big Pharmacy, and both Tibetan Noodle Coup and Chinese Noodle Coup. And despite the available 'Western' options, the most crowded breakfast stalls were those selling the traditional mix of noodles, dry or wet (soupy), soya milk, porridge and yu tiao (a kind of fried bread).

By now, I was getting rather bored of the famed Sichuan food. As a vegetarian, the only choice I had was between dry noodles or wet noodles.

There hasn't been more brutal a monopoly in the world than that deployed by Sichuan pepper in Sichuanese cuisine. This omnipresent numbing spice was like an unstoppable invasive species, dominating every other taste in the bowl. It was a welcome flavour at first, like an intruder feigning innocence. But after I had ingested as much of the spice as I had inhaled oxygen, it had destroyed my idea of the meaning of life. Despite my usual nonchalance about food, this monotony had begun to irritate me. To be fair, we had been travelling in remote towns which, because of their geography, had inherent difficulties in imagining a bountiful world for vegetarians. But as our journey got prolonged, it was getting harder and harder for

Lobo to pacify me after every meal. I would mock Sichuan's famed cuisine and extend my insults to everything about China.

I would voice criticisms like: 'When they see vegetables, they don't know what to do with them. Their main thought is, let's just stir-fry. And then, wait, let's put in some soya sauce too.'

'All they need is to broaden their minds and appreciate other spices in the world; no need to keep thinking that anything "Western" is a scheme to take over China.'

'Look at the roofs of all the temples, all the architecture has no variation, just like their spice— even that pagoda design is borrowed from Nepal or India. Their religion, zero; chess and everything else has been borrowed from India, yet they pretend as if the rest of the world never knew anything.'

Lobo would try to defend China the best she could, often pointing out that, 'Our cuisine is not world-famous for nothing. We have this, we have that. But you are now limiting all your options. You can't appreciate the pure taste of all these vegetables; you must have your cumin and garam masala and that brown gravy in everything. There's no refinement in that style of cooking.'

'There is a lot of refinement in our cuisine,' I would retort. 'What you know as Indian food is only the Mac version. Our dance, our music, everything has refined classical versions, unlike in China where dance and music has remained mostly folk in spirit.'

'That's not correct,' Lobo would fight back. 'Look at our idea of gardens or calligraphy. Classical Indian cultures had no sense of beauty in things. Our ancient literature is also far more extensive than yours.'

'That hardly matters, look at how Bollywood films are popular everywhere. No one has ever heard of a decent film from the Mainland.'

'Look at your country's performance at the Olympics.'

It could go on and on. But in actuality, food was the main topic we could argue about interminably with each other. Neither Lobo nor I claimed to be exemplary patriots. We were not even armchair patriots and given a reasonable diet, we took every chance to be critical of our own cultures. I had no interest in Bollywood films and Lobo knew less statistics than I did about China's Olympic performances. We didn't identify with any chauvinistic categorization and boasted at every opportunity about being open-minded and inquisitive about all cultures and social statuses. But somehow, we had come to a point where it had become tempting even for us to insult the 'other's' culture. I blamed it all on Sichuan pepper.

We cycled around Daocheng in the day. Unlike Yading, Daocheng was arid and sparse. The sun was strong and Lobo struggled in the thin air. We visited small villages till we realized that to continue longer might put Lobo in real danger. Lobo spent the rest of the day sleeping while I caught up on scratching my face which was itchy from my overgrown beard.

For dinner, I cajoled Lobo to try a Tibetan restaurant. Both of us had been apprehensive of partaking of Tibetan cuisine, which was famously bland and lacked variety. Tourists who typically gushed about most world cuisines as 'mouth-watering', veered away from writing glorious descriptions about Tibetan food, Filipino cuisine, perhaps, being its only other companion in this backbenchers' club. In her book *A Nomad Girl's Changing Worlds*, Sonam Doomtso mentioned a myth about Tibetan food. According to this legend, there was once an abundance of food in Tibet. One day, a nomad mother had nothing to wipe her son's bum with, so she used bread for this purpose. The gods took great offence at this and decided to punish all mankind by taking away their food, leaving some only for the dogs—disproportionate justice as is to be expected from the gods of all religions. Since then humans (actually Tibetans!) have been consuming only dog food. Despite being aware of such stories, I desperately needed a break from the Sichuan pepper monopoly and Lobo kindly obliged.

The restaurant we went to was run by two young Tibetan ladies. Though there were no other customers—Han tourists always flocked to conventional Chinese restaurants—the food was surprisingly good. I devoured rice gently fried with a generous amount of butter and a lot of capsicum and yak cottage cheese soup. Lobo, on her part, thoroughly enjoyed a sumptuous serving of dumplings served on the most elegant brass plate. The food was fragrant, diverse, decorative and tasty, well beyond our expectations.

The two ladies manning the restaurant were lively and talkative. The owner, a tall lady with handsome features said, 'Our restaurant serves food from all parts of Tibet. That's why you see such variety. At home, however, we mostly eat Han food, which is rice and stir-fried vegetables. Nowadays, I eat zanba, what you call chow mein, very rarely, only once or twice a year. We don't have Indian food here. But we have heard that Indians put a lot of effort into their cooking.'

Upon hearing that I was a vegetarian, the sisters looked rather surprised.

'Are all Indians vegetarian?' the owner asked. 'I can't imagine such a big country full of vegetarians.'

I told them that most Indians ate meat and stressed that I too used to eat meat before, all kinds of meat, from porcupine to crocodile, massive beasts to chicken. I always mentioned that to whoever enquired about my vegetarianism, as if I needed to confirm my immense capacity for cruelty.

The news that two non-Tibetan tourists were patronizing a Tibetan restaurant travelled fast and small groups of men and women dropped by to have a look at this man from India. They watched us try the food and left thereafter with a look of satisfaction. Noticing the buzz, an old Han busker came in too and sang a romantic song for us, the boy and buffalo, a toothy mariachi in tattered clothes.

For dessert, we ordered a ginseng fruit boiled in butter with sugar.

'This fruit is very special,' the owner said. 'One serving like this can increase your life by one year. So come back tomorrow for more.'

After dinner, we sat in the town square where Tibetan women were dancing in tune with music from the public sound system. But as habits are hard to change, the dance soon evolved into the sort of circumambulation that Tibetans are so used to doing around holy sites. Two young Tibetan ladies sat next to us to take a break. They looked tired and bored but when we nodded to them, their faces brightened up. The taller, darker and older of the two was called Dechen while Diki, her sister, looked exactly her opposite. We had to shout to construct a conversation over the loud music.

'These people start dancing at seven in the evening,' explained Dechen. 'Some will go on till two at night. Our dance is simple; just move your arms and limbs to the rhythm. Anyone can do it. Go try.'

When we just smiled, she said, 'And if you want to see a real dance, you should go to any of the Tibetan dance bars. Things are much wilder there. We are too old for that but maybe you two can go,' she laughed.

When I had told them that I was from India, Dechen opened up a pendant from her necklace to show the image of a lama. 'Do you know who he is?' she asked. 'He is a living Buddha. He lives in your India.'

The man didn't look like the Dalai Lama so I guessed he was the Karmapa.

'You are right,' she was delighted. 'That's why we like Indians. We like Indian movies which we get DVDs for. And we like your country as it lets our living Buddhas stay in peace.'

I recalled the controversy of the two lamas with contesting claims for the Karmapa status that had rocked the exiled Tibetan community in India. Dechen was carrying the picture of Ogyen Trinley Dorje, the one certified as the right one by most seniors from the Kagyu sect as well as the Chinese government.

'Do you love our Karmapa?' Diki asked.

'Yes,' I had to answer.

Dechen and Diki ran a shoe shop in Daocheng. They had come out for dinner and had taken the opportunity to dance in the town square, leaving the shop to their parents. Dechen was married and had one daughter, while the family was still looking for a groom for Diki.

'We Tibetans get married at an early age,' said Dechen, 'around 22 or 23, some even at the age of 15. We don't have many children, usually one, at the most, three. The harsh weather here doesn't allow us to have many. So we never needed a family control policy like the Hans.'

Only recently has this policy for Hans, limiting families to one child, been relaxed.

Upon hearing that Lobo and I were married, Dechen asked a direct, rather tactless, question, 'Why did you marry a Han? They don't have sharp features. Your Indian girls have much sharper features.'

Diki tried to salvage the situation, 'Actually, we Tibetans find Han girls pretty and tender. Many people say that my sister looks like a Han. Tibetan men want to date Han girls, but the Hans will never marry Tibetans.'

In fact, marriage between the Hans and Tibetans was a lot more prevalent than that involving any other minority in China.

Dechen asked curiously, 'Are two Indians considered married if they just exchange garlands of flowers? I saw this in a movie. Did you two just exchange flowers?'

Lobo asked the sisters about the famed macho character of the Kham men. 'Yes, Kham men are fierce, bold, courageous, always willing to fight,' Dechen said. 'But they don't do any work. My husband doesn't help at all with the child or the shop. They think it will make them girly. But nowadays things have changed. Other men, although not mine, are becoming like men from anywhere else.'

I asked them about Kham women.

'Kham women are hard-working,' said Dechen proudly. 'We can work harder than Han women. We can work in tough conditions and can survive anywhere.'

'Some of us who have got into business work less. I have more free time than my mother or my aunt, who is a nomad. Girls like us spend a lot of time doing cross-stitch. It's a favourite pastime for Tibetans. We hear that some men also do cross-stitching secretly.'

Diki showed us a photograph of her cross-stitch work, a depiction of the Potala Palace.

'She took two years to make this,' said Dechen. 'It's big, about one metre long. Isn't my sister very talented?'

Lobo asked if life had changed for the better for Tibetans, especially for women.

'Most Tibetans are rich now,' said Dechen. 'We have free education and healthcare is 70 per cent subsidized—we also get many other benefits because we are minorities. Of course, most of the businesses here are run by the Hans but the Tibetans are now making money by renting out land and picking caterpillar mushrooms, which are in high demand in China. This mushroom sells at a high price, so every year all of us Tibetans camp at the hills to collect them for a month. Mostly it's the children who gather them because they have better eyesight. Some families with hard-working children can even make 10,000 yuan in one year just by selling these mushrooms. But living in such a camp is tough, as the weather is very cold. I think the women are better off too. I definitely have more possessions than my mother. Unlike me, she started demanding things only when she became much older.'

Dechen gave her impression of India's society, 'We saw some videos of India where they showed some very poor people. But we heard that rich Indians are very wealthy. Luckily, here we don't have too rich or too poor people.'

Perhaps, Dechen was unaware of China's Gini coefficient, which was one of the worst in the world. Even among Tibetans where income inequality indeed fell after the withdrawal of the monastic aristocracy, it has been on the rise in recent years despite growing incomes for most sections of society.

Dechen showed us pictures of her seven-year-old daughter.

'She goes to school. Here, we study Mandarin, Tibetan and English. But don't ask me to talk in English. If my daughter was here, she could speak some words for you.'

They showed us pictures of distant cousins as well, one of whom had become a monk and moved to India, another who too had become a monk and gone to Singapore.

'That is why Tibetans from my parent's generation felt sad when they had girls born into their family,' Dechen said. 'I know you Hans feel that way too,' she told Lobo. 'But our reasons are completely different. Our older generation hoped that if they had a son, he could become a monk and bring a lot of merit for the family. But my parents have got used to it. They had only two of us, but we do all the work. No, Diki? If they had boys, they would just roam around all day on motorbikes or play games on the phone. What merit do you get from that?'

We didn't realize how time passed as we talked to the two sisters. But we had to fly off early in the morning the next day so we had to say goodbye. Dechen asked us the parting question which had begun to appear almost innocent and harmless by now, 'Tell me one thing. Are all Indian women dark or fair?'

The Milk Lake, Yading

Yading reflections

The Yala Mountain, Tagong

A Qiang watchtower in Zhonglu village

Audience at a beauty contest in Danba

Performers at the Danba beauty contest

Tibetan Buddhist nuns in Larung

The Larung Gar Buddhist Academy in Sertar is home to around 40,000 monks and nuns

The Yak
territory in
Tagong

A wild goat
in Yading

The statue
of Gesar in
Sertar

The Litang Monastery

A Tibetan woman
meditating with prayer
beads

Mount Chenresig

Mount Jambeyang

Pilgrims performing ritual prostrations in Larung

Ear cleaning in Chengdu

Ten

A Visa Run

The next few days were meant for insignificant battles. We had booked a flight from Daocheng to Chengdu. The airline had sent us a message the night before that the flight's timing had been advanced from its scheduled departure. This made us scramble for a shared van which could leave Daocheng at five in the morning. At 4,411 metre, the Daocheng airport was arguably the highest airport in the world. It was still dark when we reached there and the staff at the check-in counter appeared ignorant of any change in flight schedule. When we showed them the message on our phones, they just shrugged and said that the flight would be leaving at its original time, which was a good four hours later. We were furious and as was our habit in dealing with the airlines, our all-weather enemies, we created quite a scene. But the check-in ladies had nerves of steel. Without looking at us, they kept pointing at a board that asked us to call a number for customer feedback. This was exactly the opportunity that I was looking for. Just before arriving to China, I had had a string of successes in making customer complaints in Singapore—against taxi companies, e-commerce sites, airlines and restaurants. Each such campaign had resulted in glories, such as five-dollar vouchers, 50 air miles' points, a complementary dessert, small gestures to compensate for the immense mental trauma I had suffered in dealing with their well-intended if misdirected service. Inspired, I was seriously considering setting up my own back office in the Philippines from where a contract hire could regularly hurl complaints at companies and create a sweet side-income story for me. I asked Lobo to instantly dial the number and demand 5 yuan as compensation from the Chinese airline.

'We can't,' Lobo punctured my dreams. 'I don't have enough load in my phone to make a call.'

I should have known better. Lobo was always having issues with her phone. Either she would forget to carry it or its battery would be dying. My entire family was unreliable in this matter, making it rather difficult for me to nominate someone as my emergency contact. My parents never heard the phone ring and my sister's phone never received a signal. And my mother-in-law treated mobile phones the same way as snail mail, responding to messages and missed calls no earlier than a week.

To kill time at the airport, I began speed-reading

Tibetan fairy tales. These tales were all unique in one aspect; they all began at a time when 'animals and humans could understand and talk to each other.' Similar to the *Jataka Tales,* their stretched storylines purpose-designed to promote patriarchal morality bored me within five minutes. I switched to the anti-matter of Tibetan fairy tales, the *Tales of Uncle Tompa: The Legendary Rascal of Tibet.* These stories about Tibetan mischief are popular among Tibetans and Nepalese and are often their first introduction to the world of sexuality. In one story, a Tibetan family is cursed by a lama that their farm will only sprout penises. Uncle Tompa then rescues the hapless family by selling their bountiful phallus harvest to the nuns in a nunnery for a fortune! In another story, Uncle Tompa manages to get himself married into wealth. To trick the lusty groom, he attaches sheep's lungs between his legs to offer as a vagina!

The waiting time at the airport was longer than what I needed to finish the tales of Uncle Tompa. So, we decided to check out the airport shops with a steely determination to not buy anything. All that was on offer were instant noodles and caterpillar fungus. The noodles were going for 10 yuan and the fungus for anything from 30 to 200 per piece. I found it hard to spot the subtle differences between the different grades of the fungus as they all looked like miniaturized versions of a shrivelled yet upright brown penis held up by a skewer.

Caterpillar fungus was the outcome of an invasion of the bodies of ghost moth caterpillars by fungal spores. The unsuspecting bugs burrowed themselves

underground during winter. After germination, the
fungus murdered the caterpillar by consuming it
from inside and then emerged from the ground as
a thin pink stalk in spring. Known as yartsa gunbu
in Tibet, the caterpillar fungus made a relatively
late entry into the 2,500-year-old pharmacopoeia
of traditional Chinese medicine. It featured first in
Tibetan medicinal texts around the fifteenth century
and gained its reputation in China only during the
nineteenth century. Its demand grew steadily despite
blips during the Cultural Revolution, skyrocketing
after the unexpected success of Chinese long-distance
runners like Wang Junxia on the world stage during
the 1990s when the athletes and their coaches gave
the credit for their performance to caterpillar fungus.
These days, it is sold all over China and countries
with strong influence of Chinese culture as a general
cure for all conditions, from weakness to cancer,
and especially for that great obsession of traditional
Chinese medicine—male virility. Limited scientific
evidence exists for its efficacy and because of its usage
and appearance, I had a suspicion that its legend had
something to do with Uncle Tompa.

It is precisely because of such sceptical attitudes like
mine that the Chinese and the Chinese government
have been permanently offended by the 'Western
attitude' towards ancient Chinese wisdom. The 'West'
had left no chance to attack traditional Chinese
medicine, blaming it vociferously for endangering
tigers, sharks, bears and pangolins, to name a few
animals. The caterpillar fungus wasn't spared by the
'West' either, who smirked at its claims for efficacy,
criticized its arguably devastating effect on the

sensitive grasslands, and blamed it outright for inciting violence among Tibetans and between Tibetans and Hans who came to blows sporadically over the best fungus collection spots. Traditional Chinese medicine fans, to avenge such repeated insults from the 'West', had successfully managed to popularize a strange understanding of 'Western medicine' within China, as a medicinal system that deals 'only with symptoms and not the root causes.' Unfamiliar with 'Western medicine' concepts such as active ingredients or the lock and key mechanism, many Chinese have thereby fervently held on to traditional Chinese medicine with its eternal suspicion of the imbalance between 'hot' and 'cold' as the reason for most ailments. The sales pitch from traditional Chinese medicine was familiar to me. It was identical to that of Ayurveda in India whose flag-bearers had been running full-page adverts claiming how all 'Western' products are carcinogenic and only Ayurveda ticked the right boxes. In this minor clash of civilizations, the Chinese claimed one big victory when the inventors of artemisinin, a malarial treatment long prevalent in China, were awarded the Nobel Prize. Since then though, 'Western scientists' have created an alarm over growing drug resistance for artemisinin, a concept alien to traditional Chinese medicine.

But could the caterpillar fungus suffer the same fate as that of shark-fin soup? In a limited time, shark-fin soup had become an obligation in every Chinese banquet, and it disappeared just as fast, not because of the constant 'holier than thou' heckling from the 'Western media', but following campaigns by Chinese celebrities against its consumption. Despite its pockets of diversity, China, after all, was one giant monoculture where fads and habits peaked and ebbed fast and expansively.

Tibetans, anyway, seemed to be rather relaxed about the role of fungus harvesting. The ones we met said that it increased their incomes by about 20 per cent; competition for collection had meant fewer collections for each. They also mentioned that clashes over collecting domains had been mostly resolved. The Han tourists, too, appeared sangfroid about the caterpillar mummies. I had not seen anyone buying these during our entire trip though many did enquire about the price.

'Not worth it, hai zi (kid),' said an elderly man at the Daocheng airport. 'Most of these are fake anyway. I am just curious to know what others are paying for it. If I really want it, I will just look for it online.'

Back in Chengdu, Lobo needed to get her visa extended (though she was born in China, she had become a citizen of Singapore after completing her education there). To apply for the extension, Lobo needed a photograph but we couldn't find any studio near the police station which processed such requests. Lobo came up with a cunning plan. The police station was located just behind Chengdu's Tianfu Square, a place popular with local tourists for photo-ops. We stood in front of the giant Mao statue at the square and were immediately surrounded by a horde of photographers, all petite women with cameras and bags dangling from all around them. We explained that we just needed a passport picture of

Lobo. They were startled.

'But with what background?', said one lady, 'Come visit our studio. It's very near. We have a lotus pond, palace, chariots, very nice.'

'No, come with me,' said another. 'We have very nice costumes from the time of the Tang dynasty and also from the Mao period. From the novel Journey to the West also.'

'No, I just want a simple photograph, white background, no costume,' said Lobo.

'But what about your hair?' asked one of them. 'We can make a very nice bun.' She showed samples of her past business. 'You will look a Tang dynasty princess.'

'No, no,' Lobo was losing patience. 'Please understand. I just need to submit my photo to the police station.'

Eventually, we managed to get the photograph done in a musty basement dig.

We had arrived early at the police station and the employees were just getting started with their day. A policewoman was giving a motivational speech to the entire staff. Once charged up, they gave a few shouts, pumped their fists in the air, and ran to their stations. It all looked good till we saw the form for a visa extension. Lobo had to get a local address proof and then visit the police station in that area after seven days, which was impossible given our travel plans. Nonetheless, we hoped to use our charm to find a way out.

We submitted the partially filled form to a young staff member. After one glance she asked us to get the address proof and the stamp from local police. Lobo smiled and asked for an exception. The lady considered for a while and asked again for the same documents. Lobo explained why she wouldn't be able to get what the policewoman asked for.

'No, you still need the address proof and stamp from the local police,' she insisted.

At this point, Lobo flared up and questioned the logic behind this process. Before going into the police station, I had repeatedly advised Lobo not to get flustered, since I had read a few stories on the internet about foreigners getting agitated and complicating matters even further. But Lobo had forgotten my instructions completely. Such was her rage at the unmalleability of a bureaucracy she had long not dealt with but had heard enough about. She and the policewoman kept repeating the same arguments, their tempers rising in sync. It was a broken record in Mandarin, fast cascading into hopelessness. The anger soon gave away to mutual misery; Lobo wanted to talk to someone else, the lady wanted to talk to someone else too. The logjam meant trouble, but I found their interaction rather amusing. They were like a pair stuck in an unhappy arranged marriage, unable to disentangle themselves from one another, repeating the same incorrect passwords. After 10 minutes, they stopped talking. They were still facing each other but avoiding eye contact. After being entertained enough at their expense, I whispered to Lobo that there was a Plan B and broke the invisible atomic bond between these two hapless creatures.

We sat down in the lobby downstairs. I made Lobo take a few deep breaths. Right then, a middle-aged woman approached us and began talking non-stop, holding out one form after another. This lady appeared to be the guardian angel of this police station. But Lobo just kept staring at her, a blank gaze. Suddenly, with a sharp hand movement, Lobo asked her to disappear from the face of the earth, making the lady run away like a puppy that has been kicked hard.

Lobo explained, 'She was offering things like making a fake passport, or a fake hukou, a visa for Taiwan.'

The next day, Lobo followed Plan B and went for a day trip to Hong Kong to get a fresh stamp at the immigration counter, leaving me alone in Chengdu to practise my Mandarin. I visited Chengdu's multistoreyed pet market where live turtles were piled up on the floor like huge dumps of coal; kittens in crowded cages meowed at me incessantly, as if hoping desperately for a rescuer. Later in the day, I went to the Panda Centre in Chengdu. It was a futuristic yet dystopian place, an enclosure built by humans to keep animals on their own terms, a purpose-built habitat insignificant in comparison to their ancient original, meant to give us endearing views of those fortunate animals we considered adorable, and then providing inspiration to tech firms to develop terabytes of anthropomorphic emoticons.

Eleven

World's Largest Monastery and Highest Slum

We arrived in Sertar after a tortuous 14-hour bus ride of about 650 km from Chengdu, the longest so far in our trip. It was almost 10 in the night and our search for hotels became an onerous task as they all rejected us for being foreigners (hotels in China need a special licence to host foreigners). Eventually, we found a hotel next to the town square which had that cherished board with the welcoming 'Can accept aliens'. The owner, a young Tibetan man, did not want to take any risk and immediately took us to the nearby police station for the approval of the authorities before he could take our booking. That got me tense. How would the police react to the visit by an Indian man to one of the more troubled Tibetan areas, a place where a few months ago, a nun had immolated herself in the square, a popular way to express resentment against Chinese rule? A group of young policemen were eating instant noodles. All of them examined our passports like kids greedy for scrapbooks, flipping through all the pages and looking at visas from other countries from different angles. After 10 minutes of playfulness, the head of the police station returned our passports with a smile, 'One from India and one from Singapore,' he said. 'Both come to our small town. How lucky are we?'

At 4,127 m, Sertar was a shade higher than Litang, the world's highest town. The night was cold and lonely when we ventured out to get drinking water. A bunch of Tibetan men were screaming and shouting in front of the only store that was open. They were heavily drunk and once they saw us, they pounced on me.

'Leave him alone,' screamed Lobo.

The young men put their arms around me.

'No, no,' one of them said, 'We only want a photograph with him. Is that okay?'

Once they took some photos, they ran away into the darkness yodelling, deliriously happy.

The next day, we made a late start for Larung Gar, the world's largest monastery that was arguably the world's highest slum as well. It was snowing and our van skidded and swerved on the icy road. While our driver panicked, our co-passenger, a retired government employee from Guangzhou, could barely contain his excitement, 'We are so lucky that it is snowing. You two are lucky. I am lucky. We will get red against white, the red houses of the monks and the snow. It's perfect.' I chuckled at what was a photographer's outlook towards life.

The Larung monastery was opened in 1980 by Khenpo Jigme Phuntsok. The site for the monastery was so chosen because holy objects were supposedly buried underneath. Khenpo was a charismatic character, revered as the reincarnation of a teacher of the 13th Dalai Lama. The story is that he came out of his mother's womb in a meditational posture and recited Manjushri's mantra immediately thereafter[12] (many significant lamas had shown such behaviour at birth). Khenpo did much to rejuvenate Tibetan Buddhism and attracted many followers from China, particularly from the wealthy southeast. Over time, this strategy—not too dissimilar from patron-priest relationships that Tibetan monks had always engaged in with Mongol and Chinese kings—bore fruit as donations poured in from these wealthy enclaves. Khenpo envisioned Larung as a university town where monks, nuns and laypeople from all over Tibet (and China) could come and study. As the Chinese government's attitude towards religion became more relaxed, Larung spread like an amoeba over these hills to accommodate more than 10,000 residents. A formidable administrator, Khenpo was from a family of nomads. His death in 2003 at the age of 70 had a negligible impact on the running of Larung because of the effective organization he had built there, the management often comprising skilled Han followers.[13] In 2001, however, following the crackdown on the spiritual practice of Falun Gong, the People's Liberation Army moved in and demolished several houses at Larung, evicting many of its residents. Gradually, Larung's population recovered till a devastating fire in 2014 destroyed several nuns' houses. The government acted again by restricting unrestrained expansion and by moving many residents to lower slopes.

Larung was well disguised, built on hills hidden beyond hills lining the highway. But once our car wobbled along the dirt road off this highway, we saw signs of an approaching camp, similar to a refugee one. The whole place appeared a lot poorer than the rest of China that I was aware of. Stagnant pools of water had formed here and there, street urchins and dogs were roaming about aimlessly and vegetables rotted everywhere. But instead of the expected red colour, the camps were all white, nomad tents like the ones we had stayed in at Tagong.

'These people are not from here,' explained our driver. 'After one week, on the day of the full moon, there will be special prayers. These people have come for that.'

Indeed, as our van started climbing, the surroundings became tidier. Once we got out of the car, we finally realized the true scale of Larung—hills upon hills of crimson red, an endless cluster of red houses, almost identical, all tiny, just large enough to contain a small bed and a luggage bag—resembling a few thousand red Lego blocks pressed on to the earth.

A narrow paved road twisted and turned along the hills for some distance. Countless unpaved tracks sew up this settlement and we wandered aimlessly through this red maze dripping from the snow melt. Once we reached the top of a hill, we could finally see the gigantic slum in its entirety, an ocean of tin roofs, each held in place by large stones.

As the sun climbed higher, the sky cleared up and the blanket of grey was lifted. Many monks climbed up to the large colourful vats that had sprung up at many places to burn twigs for their smoke-offering rituals. The houses were now bright red, glittering with their tiny windows reflecting the sunlight in tiny ways. They had been built in bricks or wood and then painted in uniform ochre.

A group of monks were building a new house. Each monk had a wooden backpack, like a small open drawer, tied to his back to carry six to eight bricks. We talked to one of them who showed us inside the space they were constructing. Most of the houses were cubicles that went 2 metre in each dimension, with just enough space for a small bed, a stove and a chimney. There was no heating and the showers and the toilets were communal, separate for males and females. It was hard to imagine any kind of luxury in such a state of living. Larung was a place purely designed for faith or an escape from desperation.

'It takes five or six days to build such a house here,'

the young monk explained. 'You pay 7,000-8,000 yuan to buy something like this. The rate gets cheaper as one goes higher up in the mountains—that's where the children stay. Earlier, you could get a place for even 3,000 yuan. But nowadays, everything is expensive.'

In Larung, prices for construction, repair, transport, healthcare and other public work were regulated and earlier we had spotted a rate card for construction and repair activities, authorized by the Larung Financial Committee's Pricing Department.

We asked the monk about the abundance of soggy biscuits and rotten food that we had seen on the rooftops.

'People just throw things out of their kitchens,' the monk smiled. 'Or they feed birds and cats to gain merit and then forget to clean up.'

They were all immigrants here, coming from across the Tibetan–Qinghai plateau and also from China. They were of all ages, from 5 to 100. These days, there are perhaps around 4,000 to 5,000 residents in Larung—no one was certain (official restrictions apparently limited the number of residents to a maximum of 2,000). Nearly half of the inhabitants were women. About 10 to 20 per cent of the residents were Hans. The paved road split the settlement by gender—the nuns stayed to the right, the monks to the left. There were laypeople also; they ran small shops or begged the tourists for money.

As the weather became better, more Han tourists arrived. They came out of the vans brandishing giant cameras and began taking snaps of everything. The monks we were talking to hid their faces and looked away. We left them to visit the children's quarters. We saw young faces peeping at us from behind the walls. When spotted, the youngest attempted to shoot me down with a slingshot.

'Tashi delek,' I surrendered and raised my arms.

They broke into laughter. They were a group of four, between 5 and 8 years old, who shared that tiny house. I asked them where they came from and they just said,

'Here.'

From inside the house, a mature voice, perhaps the oldest in the group, scolded them and called them inside.

We went to the main temple where hundreds of laypeople were either circumambulating the temple's buildings or repeatedly prostrating themselves. They had furrowed faces, deeply tanned skins, long hair, dirty clothes, dark glasses, hats, and a general air of 'we have never showered' about them. Perhaps they had all turned up fresh from the movie set of a Spaghetti Western. When we joined the circumambulating group, the pilgrims got distracted by my beard. A group of elderly people asked us to sit down with them. They couldn't speak any Mandarin so they just smiled. More people approached us to say 'Tashi delek'. A young couple goaded their baby to offer us the milk she was drinking. One scruffy man attempted to sell his rosary beads to me.

Once the crowd cleared away, I spotted two nuns who had just arrived at the temple. They had closely cropped hair and were perhaps in their fifties, although Tibetans usually appear much older for their age. They walked barefoot and their faces hinted of complete innocence and a certain spirit that knew no complexity in life. As soon as they reached the temple grounds, they dropped on to the floor and began doing prostrations. I noticed the colour of their palms, an inhuman brown from a lifetime of falling on the ground in the quest for *nirvana*. Radiant smiles blossomed on their faces showing happiness that was shockingly alien to me.

We visited the medicine shop that stocked a large collection of Tibetan, Chinese as well as 'Western' medicine. We spoke to the resident Tibetan doctor, a man in his thirties who appeared a little bored with his circumstances.

He said, 'I hardly get any complicated cases here, mostly women's problems. Flu is also common because there are so many old people here. And for the Han monks, they always get altitude sickness. I just diagnose by checking a patient's pulse. Where serious cases are concerned, we send the patients to Sertar.'

We asked him how the monks paid for the medicines.

'They pay,' the doctor said. 'All of them get an annual stipend from the temple donations. They pay from there.'

'And by the way,' he continued, 'I also see a lot of

infants. Many children born out of wedlock are left here.'

Outside the medicine shop, we met a Han monk. He was in his eighties but appeared strong, almost Neanderthal. He used to be a farmer in Liaoning, a northeastern province of China, and he was delighted to hear that Lobo was from the same province.

'My daughter also lives here,' he said with a laugh that was a constant on his face. 'But of course, her house is on the other side of the road. I was uneducated. I learnt to read only after coming here. Earlier I understood nothing. Now that I am older and can read, I understand a lot more about Buddhism.'

'I bought a house here three years earlier. Also, we get money for attending classes here,' he laughed. 'I miss most of them but whenever I feel short of money, I go and attend a few classes.'

We asked him if life was hard during winter.

'Yes,' he said. 'But you must know that winters in the northeast are not any better. I was always poor so we had no heating.'

A group of young Tibetan women broke into our conversation to beg for money. Instead of asking us, they began pestering the monk.

'You should be ashamed to ask me,' he said as he chased them away. 'You should be the one paying me to gain some merit.'

It was getting late for lunch. There were a few restaurants at the square where the visitors were dropped off. We settled at a small restaurant selling Sichuan food there. A young Tibetan monk came up to me,

'Hello, how are you?' he spoke perfect English.

Jigme and his friend sat down with us for lunch. Jigme had a sturdy build and a perfect smile. He wore thick glasses and spoke in a gentle voice. His friend was a layperson who was too shy to speak to us.

'I am from Dege in eastern Tibet,' he said. 'I came here in 2008 and then again in 2011. In between, I went to India, to Bodhgaya. When I came back, I bought one of the small houses here.'

Jigme spent most of the day studying.

'Over the last 1,200 years, Tibetans went to much greater depths to expand Buddhist philosophy, which they originally took from India. So there is a lot to read. Every day, I get up at seven in the morning. It is too cold to wake up before that,' he said, smiling. 'I cook my food and then go for classes. There are a lot of classes. But, this month is the time when the monks take some time off from studies to meditate three to four hours every day. Some are even not eating during this period. I have not reached that stage yet even though I am at a reasonably high level studying Tantra.'

We recalled the printouts posted on the doors of some monk's quarters, 'I am meditating. Only knock if really necessary.' Special hotline numbers were also pasted on key intersections, to be dialled in case of an emergency if the concerned officials were not available because of their meditational obligations during this period.

'There are frequent exams,' said Jigme, 'Every month there are tests, written and oral, and debates. If you top at the end of the year, you get a gold medal, then silver, then bronze, others get something made of glass. If you fail, you stay in the same class. You must consider this place not as a monastery but more like a university. Here, you can learn Tibetan literature, medicine, astronomy and culture. With all this, our day typically ends at eleven.'

I asked him about career opportunities.

'Most just move on after staying here a few years and then join as monks in some other temple. Only some who want to become teachers stay for long periods to learn more. As for me, I want to stay on. I want to explain to the rest of the world my knowledge and understanding of Buddhism.'

He talked about life in such a slum.

'Here, life is good, even though so many people live so closely together. There are many rules to keep things orderly; maybe too many. But this whole place is very democratic because every proposal for a new rule has to be put to vote. This can lead to funny situations like we had once over whether we can wear vests. Kham and Amdo Tibetans like to wear vests but the central Tibetans don't so it was put to a vote and it was decided that no one will be allowed to wear vests from now on. But there are so many young people here. If they are always restricted, they will revolt so we don't always punish them and everyone is equal before law.'

I was naturally curious about the interaction between the young monks and the nuns.

'The monks and nuns can only meet during noon and that too in common areas. Yet, every year we do hear of a couple or two who suddenly disappeared,' he laughed. 'But, you see there are a lot more young monks than young nuns here. Most of the males here were sent by their parents at a very young age. I came here at the age of 14.' That meant Jigme was only 21. He sounded too mature for his age.

'But regarding the females,' Jigme continued, 'there are not many young ones. Most are elderly, people abandoned by their families.'

I asked him if the government rolled in from time to time.

'Yes, officials do,' he whispered. 'But nowadays they largely leave us alone. Unless, they find an excuse. Like after the fire, they forced most old people to move to government-made housing down below. They said it will be easier to rescue them in case there was an emergency but the old now find it hard to come up to the classes. The Chinese government doesn't want this place to grow too big and they don't want the old and young to mingle. This is the Communist way of doing things—no discussion, just acting on what they think is good for others.'

After lunch, we walked through the female quarters. There were notices outside every ladies' toilet proclaiming, 'Gentlemen, you will lose merit if you enter the women's toilet.'

We walked inside a nunnery. It had many chambers and we entered some of the classrooms. Their walls were gaudily decorated with Tibetan-style paintings. There were no classes on that day but a lot of isolated activities were happening at different places within the nunnery. In one chamber, 10 nuns with shaved heads sat in a circle reading mantras. At another place, 15 of them sat in near-complete darkness, rolling balls of zanba. The nuns appeared guarded but we were impressed by the scale of the operations. Along one corridor, a baby-faced Tibetan girl was sitting with a basket full of cowrie shells. She was churning them with her hand and then putting them one by one into a bowl while counting. Upon seeing us, she gave a big smile. We sat down for a chat, happy to find a more welcoming nun.

'This is a way of meditation,' Sangye said. 'Today there are no classes. So I have time to do this.'

Sangye came from Yushu, a prefecture inhabited mostly by Tibetans in the southwestern Qinghai province of China, and was only 18 years old.

'Every day we wake up early to cook,' she said. 'Then there are morning prayers. Then we have seven to eight hours of classes. In the evening, we have debates. We have three meals a day. Whenever we have some free time, we pray or meditate.'

Sangye's father had died after being struck by lightning a few years back. Soon after, her uncle dropped her to the monastery.

'It is better here,' Sangye said. 'As good as it could get for me perhaps. At home, they would make me work all day and night. I had become so thin.'

It was not clear if Sangye had rebelled and was, therefore, sent here. Tibetan women who became nuns at a young age were often forced to choose the institution to escape from bad marriages, widowhood or domestic violence. For such women, not only could life in a nunnery be better but also provided the promise of a better reincarnation. Despite that, nuns had to live as second-class citizens in the monastic hierarchy of Tibetan Buddhism, having to face several micro-aggressions, such as sitting behind monks in gatherings to outright denial of permission to be ordained at higher ranks such as the bhikkhuni. With many 'Western' females becoming nuns and also through rising consciousness among the Tibetan nuns themselves, this issue has been raised in Tibetan establishments around the world. The Dalai Lama showed his support for equal rights by accepting that his successor could be a woman but he then went on to say in the same interview that such a female leader has to be 'very, very attractive' to be of any use. Larung had been a pioneer in that sense, being the first institutions to allow women to become khenpos (something like a PhD). And a few months after our trip, a group of nuns began running study sessions on feminism and published books and magazines on important female figures in Buddhism.[14]

We left Sangye and entered a dark, elongated hall. At its centre, there was a panel of large statues of the three Dharma kings, looking at me with their big angry eyes. They were surrounded by fake plastic trees with tiny spiral lights around their twigs, blinking in pink, green and blue. Soporific chants of *Lama Chenno* streamed out of the stereo. We sat down in one corner and fell asleep in this electronic paradise.

We came back to the main temple in the evening. There, we spotted three young Han monks sitting on a broken door panel and counting beads. We went over to have a chat. One of them, Lin, was very frail and spoke in a nasal voice. Jian, the second person, spoke in a gentle, articulated manner and offered us to sit with them. Kang, the third man and perhaps the youngest, was an introvert, speaking out only when he couldn't resist any more. Lin had been here for over three years. The other two had come the year before. Based on our discussions, I classified the three men as Jian: the idealist, Lin: the pragmatist and Kang: the sceptic. All three of them were from Heilongjiang, China's northernmost province.

'I don't know why,' said Lin, 'Somehow many Dong Bei (northeastern) monks have come over here.'

Jian, the reformer, asked us, 'You see so many beggars here nowadays. What do you think of them? We are worried they are spoiling the monastery's image. What can we do as a monastery to prevent this?'

Lin, the pragmatist, scolded him, 'Why does it bother you? Leave it to the authorities.'

Kang lashed out, 'They will make the whole system collapse.'

Noticing Kang's rising temper, Jian changed the topic, 'You are from India. Tell us, why did Buddhism decline in India while it is much better preserved in China?'

Lin answered on my behalf, 'Buddhism was never big in India, it was only popular among a few important rulers but never among the whole population.'

I added whatever little I knew—the absorption of Buddhist elements in later-day Hinduism, the breakdown of Buddhist empires into smaller kingdoms that gradually embraced Hinduism and the general revival in Hinduism brought about by strong religious leaders like Shankaracharya.

Jian looked satisfied, 'Well, whatever it is. The fact is that although China and India have tough relations now, we will always respect India for bringing in Buddhism.'

In his zeal for reform, Jian asked us another toughie, 'So tell us. You have travelled around the world. What can Buddhism do to be as successful as Christianity? Even in China, Christians are getting stronger by the day.'

Kang lashed out again, 'They have money. You don't have any. It's that simple.'

Lobo provided her theory, 'I think Buddhism is more inner-centric and not action-oriented like Christianity and that's why it hasn't succeeded. Look at how the Christians organize community activities. Perhaps monks should get more involved in volunteerism.'

The northeastern monks, except Kang, looked very impressed.

Jian said, 'That was a revelation. You are like Guanyin, the bodhisattva of compassion, who just showed us the way.'

Kang put out another of his one-liners, 'I can only do as much as I can afford.'

Before we left, I asked them about the future of Buddhism in China, given that it was getting increasingly pop and tacky with an emphasis on mega shrines and Buddha parks with high entry prices and mandatory cable car rides.

Lin replied, 'It's sad but it's true. It is getting commercialized but you have to understand that's what the government is trying to do. That's not the way we common people practise Buddhism. In any case, there is a growing interest in Buddhism. The pressure of the materialistic life in China is pushing more people towards religion. I think Buddhism will eventually succeed in China. The last 50 years were just an anomaly.'

We couldn't find any other passenger to share the ride back to Sertar as most of the Chinese tourists had already left. But other drivers joined us for company.

One of them tried to speak some English with me. He got mocked heavily by his companions. Another sang a few lines from the Bollywood song *Kuch Kuch Hota Hai,* invariably the first words from India learnt by people in developing countries.

We asked the drivers about Larung. Rambo, the one who spoke broken English, said, 'Life is so good there. They don't have to worry about money like us. I wish I had no responsibility like them. Then I could just say a few prayers and enjoy life.'

'But wasn't life tough in these small shelters with tough discipline and communal toilets?' I asked.

'You may think living here is tough but people get used to it. After two or three days, you don't care about discipline or toilets. Look at us, if we didn't meet you, this poor driver would have gone without any income today,' Rambo said.

He put on some loud music, a Kanye West song.

'Here, this will keep you entertained,' Rambo said.

'But these monks must be good for your business,' I said.

'Yes, they are. That's why laypeople like us followed them here. But they also bring in problems. Did you hear about the fire? It was because one nun forgot about the fire she had lit in her kitchen. Four hundred homes were affected. You can't even trust them to take care of themselves. How can they take care of all of us Tibetans and mankind?'

'Tibetans?' the driver of our van spoke for the first time. He had only been laughing thus far on hearing Rambo's English. 'Rambo,' he asked with a smirk, 'You think they have time to take care of Tibetans? They are too busy with Han donors. You will see the senior monks tonight if you go to any expensive restaurant in Sertar, enjoying life with their Han followers. Go to a Han restaurant because Han followers can't have Tibetan food.'

He looked at us, 'Our monks follow the Hans to these restaurants because in Larung you can't cook meat.'

Everyone began laughing, clapping and screaming hysterically.

Monks and monasteries had been long vilified by the Communist Party of China as the source of many ills in Tibetan society—its feudal nature (monasteries were the biggest landowners in many regions of Tibet), institutionalized slavery (indentured labour) for many laypeople, ill-treatment of women, sexual abuse of children (as monk's companions) and the general lag in material advancement. The exiled Tibetan community denied these allegations or protested that reforms were already underway before the PLA moved in. Even neutral experts couldn't arrive at a unanimous verdict.

The history of Tibet, therefore, continued to remain more uncertain than for most societies, serving only as tinder to the conflict. But I was surprised to hear such strong words from Rambo and his friends as

Tibetans were generally known to revere their lamas and monks. Perhaps it was just the laypeople's angst about monks who they expect to be living in austere, abject conditions.

Twelve

A Sky Burial

The next day, we went back to Larung to attend a sky burial. Around 50 Han tourists, all wearing face masks, had already gathered for this spectacle. Unlike the one at Litang, the sky burial site in Larung had been done up for tourists. Visitors were greeted by a huge rock-cut edifice, titled 'The Temple of Death'. Rather strangely, the sculptures in this temple's grounds tried to mimic an Aztec sacrifice. When I commented about the oddity to another tourist, he smiled, 'What do you expect? We are Chinese. We only know how to build infrastructure. We can't understand other people's culture. So we built a train to Tibet and will now make a tunnel through the Everest. But we don't understand Tibetans.'

The burials were carried out in a small enclosure

outside this touristy temple complex. Strangers were barred from entering this place. Vultures had already assembled in large numbers on the slopes. Somehow they knew that it was time, so they were getting restless, flying low and flapping their huge wings. These birds were enormous, the biggest I had seen. Vultures were considered inauspicious in our hometown. Shakun, the Bengali word for vulture, had a potent symbolism for us because of its proximity to Shakuni, the most reviled character in the *Mahabharata*. When I was a child, an injured vulture had fallen into our backyard one day. It had been sitting motionless for the whole day. Taking pity on it, we gave it some water to drink in the evening. Thirsty as it was, it extended its long neck and reached for us with what seemed like one last effort. That sudden motion and its dreadful eyes scared me so much that I ran away. The vulture survived and flew away the next morning; so I was told by my parents. Or was it dispatched by the municipality to an incinerator? Contrarily, in Tibetan belief systems, vultures were the kings of the birds because they flew so high; therefore, being devoured by them could ensure a person a higher reincarnation.

Who was the man whose body was on offer today? We couldn't see who it was for the body was well hidden between the monks and the family as they went inside the enclosure. There was a signal and then the birds swooped in, in number of perhaps 50 or 100. I had heard that if a person had a high moral character, the vultures would first eat away the skin of his face. And if someone had been really evil, the hungry beasts wouldn't even touch the body. Some tourists turned back, 'Ah, there is nothing to see. What's the point?'

Even I did not feel any urge to witness the burial,
having already read a body part by body part account
by Ma Jian in his book *Stick Out Your Tongue* (it was
banned by Chinese authorities for portraying Tibetan
culture in a negative light). Yet, I was curious to know
if the birds considered the dead man a good or bad
person. I noticed that the family members were
sobbing. Since Tibetans resisted crying after a person's
death because of their belief that it confused the soul
and complicated its departure, the tears were perhaps
a sign that the birds' posthumous verdict had gone
against the unfortunate person.

After the vultures had had their first taste, the
body was usually cut into smaller pieces to help the
birds finish off the more difficult-to-eat parts. I felt
a tingling on my skin as I thought, what if the body
parts were mine? I touched my cheeks and arms.
For a living person, it was awfully scary to imagine
being eaten away by an animal or bird after death.
But it made perfect spiritual sense to Tibetans who
believed in reincarnations and the non-significance
of the body after death. It was also a perfectly
rational choice by the living, given that firewood for
cremations was scarcely available and burials were
difficult in these thin-crust highlands. I was also
intrigued by the elaborate belief system created by
Tibetan culture to cope with death. The *Bardo Thodol*
(Tibetan Book of the Dead) made death seem such an
inviting proposition if only for the chance to see the
visions promised during the journey of the spirit after
death, the fantastic wrathful and merciful gods and
goddesses like the White Cemetery Goddess holding
a corpse as a club, Chandali, the pale yellow goddess,

tearing off and munching the head of a human corpse, the five blood-drinking fathers, the black fox-headed goddess savouring an intestine, and all sorts of animal-headed deities. And wasn't it tempting to try out the tricks recommended by *Bardo Thodol* to avoid reincarnation? It recommended floating away from the doors of an open womb or closing the womb-door through techniques involving meditation on deities like the Avalokiteswara, the bodhisattva of compassion, or by avoiding getting in between the mating pair of yab-yum (father-mother).[15] The *Bardo Thodol* was read to a person on a deathbed to assist his spirit in making the right choices after death. I had read it with no one in mind, and it was unlikely that anyone would read it for me.

It was all over in 10 minutes. The family left. The monks left. The remaining tourists lingered on for a while hoping for some more action and then left after taking some more photographs of the out-of-place sculptures. We were then alone with the rag-collectors and the vultures. Fearless, the birds inched in towards us. They looked unsatisfied and perhaps were expecting to feast on us. I recalled that in India, rapid urbanization had significantly diminished the population of this species. As such, the Parsis of India, who followed a similar burial practice with their Towers of Silence, had to import vultures and deploy solar reflectors for faster decomposition of their dead. But out here, there seemed to be too many vultures and too few deaths. One bird came very close and looked at me ominously. I went back to the days when the Tibetan fairy tales had been written, when animals and men understood each other. I imagined the bird was asking me, 'When is your turn? Why not now? Why do you want to carry on longer? Didn't you just see? You are nothing. Ask us, we know the skies and the universe. But I could eat your face first and make the world believe that you were a noble man. But what's the point? After all, some day we will also eat those who will care to remember you. Give your flesh to us. Now or a few years later, what difference does it make? The world is too old and you are never too young.' It rose up in the air, flying straight towards me. I could feel the wind from its wings.

Thirteen

The Land of Gesar

We loved Sertar. It was neat. It was small. The entire town could be walked through in 20 minutes, the valleys, stupas and monasteries providing the directions. There was a comfortable Tibetan restaurant at the edge of the town where we could spend a lifetime sipping endless cups of sweet milk tea from a giant brass teapot. At the other end of the town was an old white stupa where we could also spend a lifetime people-watching in the balmy sun, observing new pilgrims who turned up every day. In the evenings, we would go to the town square hoping that people would come to dance. But no one came other than the familiar group of young louts who would always want to take photographs with me. Our friendly policemen kept looking all day for any sign of flames as Sertar was a hotspot for self-immolations in opposition to Han rule.

During the day, the town square was haunted by drivers looking for custom. Every time we passed by them, they would reconfirm our travel plans with us. They were playful and relaxed, our friends in this new city. A driver from Lhasa, who had been stuck here for more than a week, spent time watching 'Just for Laughs' gags on his phone. When we asked him what kind of town Lhasa was, he would give out a sigh, 'Don't remind me of Lhasa. It is the best city in the world.'

One driver from Kangding told us, 'The people of Sertar are the craziest. They are the most religious and the most extreme. People here are known to go to the temples and set their fingers on fire as a sacrifice to gain merit.'

One day, a group of drivers took us to show us what they said was a 'wonder'. We walked together to a monastery under construction. At its entrance, there was a strange mechanical contraption of giant prayer wheels connected to each other by a complicated network of gears and chains.

'Look what this board says,' the drivers told us.

In Mandarin, it said:

World's first such rolling structure of 100-syllable mantras.
Formed of 108 rolling charms, each has 0.16 billion 100-syllable mantras in the inner side...
Special soft print technique ensures the paper is

continuous and hence has complete merit...
*Has both engine rotation and manual rotation
mode...*
*Walking one round around this is equivalent to
chanting the 100-syllable mantras 17.28 billion
times. If you rely on machine rotation then in one
day and one night, you can finish chanting of the
100-syllable mantras 270 trillion times ... this
merit lasts long and is continuous....*
*The massive scale of the chamber and the charm,
the vast number of mantras, and the highly
difficulty level of technology, are all considered
best in the world.*
*Since the day this was built, whenever someone
rotates it or even the slightest wind strokes it, it
will benefit countless people ...*
*This merit is like the mercy of Buddhas, no place is
too far to reach and it is eternal....*

'The government is building this for us Tibetans.'

'Will people come here?' I asked.

'Why not? See that old monk is already walking
around it. We Tibetans will fall for anything.'

This was another sign of the government's attempt
to win the hearts and minds of Tibetans and what
better way to do it than provide a shortcut to gain
merit. Wasn't the Communist Party especially good
with playing such games of large numbers? The sight
of the turning wheels and the men walking around it
left me rather disturbed, thinking how easily religion
went to bed with the powers that be.

In its quest to win hearts and minds, the government had also been promoting local legends, that of Gesar in particular. It was in and around Sertar that the legendary King Gesar went around destroying evil, his adventures being captured in the world's longest song, *The Epic of Gesar.* A massive museum dedicated to Gesar had been built in Sertar and statues of Gesar and his horse could be seen at key intersections of the town. The historicity of Gesar is debatable and the collection of the museum, therefore, is limited to paintings of scenes from the epic and an imposing cavalcade of freshly cast statues of Gesar in bronze in the courtyard. When we visited the museum, there were only two other people inside. They looked like Tibetan officials on a work trip. In hushed tones, they discussed every painting with great interest.

When we mentioned Gesar to our driver friends, they would always break into yodelling. Even today, nomads sang scenes from the epic when they got together at night around a fire. *The Epic of Gesar* remained a living tale and singers were adding adventures to the already long story even to this date. Serta also held an annual Gesar Rap festival.

The first Chinese translation of *The Epic of Gesar* was written by Professor Ren Naiqiang, a Han academic from Sichuan (he was also the man who made the first map of Tibet). Fascinated by Tibetan culture, the professor learned a Kham dialect and went on to marry a Tibetan woman. During his wedding festival, local singers sang The Epic of Gesar. Professor Ren spent a good amount of time during his own wedding translating the songs.[16] I was certain that he had chosen his life partner only to hear The Epic of Gesar on his own terms.

We left Sertar for Danba, the valley of watchtowers and beautiful Tibetan women. We were skipping the towns of Dege, home to the largest Tibetan scriptures' printing institute, Garze, a famed Tibetan town, and Miyaluo and Bippenggou, known for their autumn scenery. Since the route from Sertar to Danba was not high on demand, we could only get a shared taxi up to Bamei. Our fellow passenger was a Han lady in her 30s who seemed to be enamoured by Eastern spirituality. She was dressed like a true Chinese hippie in a flowing red linen shirt, baggy colourful trousers and lots of beads.

'I am Radhe Ma,' she introduced herself. 'I am a yoga teacher in Shanghai. I have been to your India. I learnt yoga from Guru Siddhantaji in Rishikesh. Don't you know him?'

She seemed to be one of those nice people on earth who are instantly unlikeable. She had been dropped off at Sertar's town square by a group of monks. They had given her two rolls of thanka paintings which she carried rather clumsily as they rolled over on the car's dashboard from one side to another, causing a lot of inconvenience for the young Tibetan driver.

Upon hearing that I didn't know any yoga guru, Radhe Ma (also the name of a legendary medieval era devotee of the Hindu god, Krishna) lost interest in us. But she made one more attempt to befriend us by playing a new age Punjabi song on her mobile that kept repeating the word 'Sadguru' (holy teacher) over a mellow lounge rhythm. Lobo didn't understand a thing and I put on an expression of a bored Egyptian mummy. Disappointed, Radhe Ma attempted a conversation with Rabten, the driver.

'So tell me some stories from your religion,' she demanded, almost leaning on to Rabten.

Rabten replied that he didn't know of any.

'Really?' she was surprised. 'Didn't you recognize the monks who had just come to see me off? I was learning Buddhism from them. Those monks are very senior, very important. Anyway, tell me some lessons taught in Buddhism.'

'I don't know them,' Rabten said with a glum face. 'I don't know any lessons.'

'Do you want some chocolate?' Radhe Ma asked. 'Wait, you are driving, I will help you.' She unwrapped the chocolate and put it in Rabten's mouth. 'It is nice, right.'

Rabten didn't seem to enjoy the taste.

The condition of our road worsened as it lost its asphalt cover within an hour of leaving Sertar. We bumped from stone to stone as we turned and turned along the mountain cliffs, the thankas throwing tantrums on the dashboard. At every turn, Radhe Ma would lunge onto Rabten's shoulders—he was the Khampa man and Radhe Ma was the damsel in distress. After an hour of spin-drying, we hit a fine road and from there on it was a smooth ride to Bamei. Radhe Ma began her research into Tibetan Buddhism again,

'So many monks. So many monks at Larung,' she said. 'You guys are so lucky to live there.'

Rabten said, 'I live in Kangding.'

'Then why are you going back? You should have waited till the festival was on.'

'Yeah, but I have to make a living.'

'We Hans are spoiling you. You Tibetans have learnt to say this only from people from Beijing and Shanghai.'

Radhe Ma put on a mocking voice, 'We have to make a living. Everybody has to make a living. There's no time for inner peace. I am sad that Tibetans will become like us soon.'

'Anyway,' Rabten said, 'Maybe half the pilgrims camping at Larung for the festival are fakes, spies sent in by the Han government to keep track of what is happening. Whenever there is a big gathering of Tibetans, the Hans are scared.'

'Really, you think the Hans are really that bad? The government is doing so much for the economy of you people.'

There was a pause. Then, perhaps emboldened by Radhe Ma's patronizing of Tibetans and knowing that we were foreigners, Rabten screamed out, 'I hate them. I really hate them. It's just not fair!'

After that, the car became a lonely place. No one talked to each other. Rabten did not explain what was not fair—the continuous insults targeted at the Dalai Lama, the growing share of the Hans in Tibetan economy, or the Sinification of an ancient society. Even if Tibet was independent, its culture and economy would have been vulnerable to the giant next door that churned out cultural and material trends with an intensity that Tibetans could never match. Yet, Tibet's landscape and scattered population had thus far applied natural brakes to this process, thus preserving its culture a lot more than what was experienced by Manchuria, a region that had become indistinguishable from the rest of China. Could the solution for the Sino-Tibetan conflict be rather straightforward then—sustained commitments to talk to the other side, respect for Tibetan culture and its icons, more support to cope with the Chinese economic order, greater flexibility, and less corruption and high-handedness—many of these being things that would do a lot of good to not just Tibet but the whole of China. This was possible if China could avoid considering any concession on its part as a throwback to the weaknesses and humiliations of the nation during the late Qing dynasty. This was possible if the exiled community recognized that ground realities in Tibetan areas were vastly different from their frozen memories of the miserable conflict-laden 1960s and that the material gains for many Tibetans in the recent years have been real. But as railway lines and all-weather roads twisted through the mountains of this sparsely populated land and questions arose about what would happen after the death of the Dalai Lama, the conflict—so far low on violence and high on mistrust—was entering an uncertain phase. The increasing interest in Tibetan Buddhism by the Hans was only adding another uncharted dimension to this maze. Donations by wealthy patrons from southeast China had led to a recent revival in Tibetan Buddhism—supporting the renovation of Tibetan monasteries, construction of extensions, running of large charities, and even opening of their branches in eastern China. The exiled community, on the other hand, often relied on Western donations. The future of the two Tibetan communities—one in exile and one at home—could very well be shaped by the sentiments and interests of their two distinct groups of patrons.

We passed through the valley of Luohe where the sun shone bright and the autumn leaves gathered all the yellow in the world. It was four in the evening when we said goodbye to Rabten and Radhe Ma. I wondered how the rest of the journey would be for both of them. They had stopped talking after Rabten's sudden outburst against the 'Han' government. Radhe Ma had also stopped leaning on his shoulders. She was perhaps then no different from most Chinese who even if highly critical of government institutions and low-level government staff in private, often wholeheartedly believed in their government propaganda, whether it was the demonization of the Japanese, or the justness of the nine-dash line, or the theory of Hans liberating oppressed Tibetans whose deposed leader, the Dalai Lama, was the undiluted devil.

At Bamei, we looked for a car that could take us to
Danba. The drivers of the town converged on us and
began shouting 'Danba, Danba' to see if any other
passengers were interested. It was only a two-hour
ride but as it happened in these areas, few travelled
after the early morning. We were, therefore, forced to
spend a night in Bamei. We checked into the Grand
Hotel. Despite its name, the floor was cracked and
its clocks had long stopped bothering to keep time.
There were no other guests at the hotel and most of its
rooms were now taken up by the Tibetan family that
ran the place. To make the most of these rooms, the
parents had also given birth to many children. When
showing us our room, the daughter-in-law of the
family beat the beds hard to drive away all the dust
that had gathered from the time of Padmasambhava,
the eighth-century Buddhist master from India, also
known as Guru Rinpoche. There was nothing to do at
Bamei but it was a full moon night and we killed time
by watching the Yala Mountain reflecting its beauty
back to the moon.

Fourteen

The Valley of Beauties

Wasn't that Sitting Bull? He had put on a bit of weight since his fearsome days and had taken up a new job, driving a shared van from Bamei to Danba. The legendary Lakota warrior was in a permanent good mood, 'International friend,' he told me with a big grin. 'You have to wait. There are only 15 of us and I need to fill up five more places. I know I am being a bad person. But how else can I feed my old woman?'

We waited for an hour and then Sitting Bull came jumping with glee. Behind him was a villager struggling with several gunny bags. 'You should all thank him,' he told us. 'With all this luggage, I will count him as five.'

Sitting Bull neatly tucked in the giggling man so

that he could fit into any available space in between all his gunny bags.

Our fellow passengers included three elderly women who were dressed in ethnic costumes, wearing elaborate jewellery. Lobo asked if they dressed like that every day. One of them explained, 'No, no. We are all going to watch the Danba Beauty Contest. It has become a custom for everyone who attends the contest to dress well.'

We were not aware of what this event was.

'International friend,' said Sitting Bull. 'You are a lucky man. You come here and our region lines up all the beauties for you. Pay me a bit more for the ride.'

The women of Danba were famous in China for their beauty. The tourism industry had latched on to this reputation and marketed the region as the Danba Beauty Valley. At chinatravel.com, I had found the following description of the ladies of Danba:

No matter they stay in the village or walk out of the mountain, they rarely make up or dress up with colorful clothes. They are very industrious and hardworking people. In spite of cold wind or torrid sun, as long as they make a little wash or dress, their glamorous body shape, charm, elegance, and beauty of health will be hard to hide. Their soft and fine skin transmits the gentle shine of jade.[17]

Legend has it that a long time ago, when humans and animals could still understand one another, a phoenix flew to Mount Murdo, the holiest mountain in the Danba region, and then split into thousands of beautiful ladies. Their lineage continues till today. To make the most of this distinction, the Danba Beauty Contest was conceptualized as the institutionalized response to brand the region for tourists and also for the locals to have some fun. Lobo asked the middle-aged ladies if they were contestants themselves.

'No, no,' the women giggled. 'We are too old.'

One of our co-passengers warned us, 'Ask our international friend not to have too high expectations. All the beauties of Danba have already left, to work in the cities.'

Danba had been famous all over China for another reason, for the legend of the Eastern Queendom, an empire run by a lineage of hereditary queens, where women ruled the roost and men served merely as footnotes. The queendom was perhaps a historical reality as references to it were found in the records from both the Sui and the Tang dynasty periods. Some Chinese even believe that in the classic Journey to the West, a sixteenth-century Chinese novel, it was the region of Danba that Tripitaka, the character loosely based on Hiuen Tsang (the Chinese Buddhist monk, traveller and scholar), passed through on his way to obtain Buddhist scriptures from India. In that particular episode in the book, the queen and Tripitaka almost fell in love, an event that would have eliminated his motivation to continue further on to India. In the end, Tripitaka's vows of bachelorhood prevailed and millions of Chinese sobbed watching this heartbreaking episode in the massively popular

TV show based on the book. There is, however, a dispute over whether there had been one queendom or two in the east, or even whether one of them eventually migrated to form the other as some historians argue. In recent times, a dispute had also erupted over the precise location of the capital of the queendom as three villages around Danba— Jiazu, Zhonglu and Suopo—all laid claims, partly in expectation of tourism dollars; a low-intensity tussle not too different from that over the claims of being Shangri-La.[18]

On our way to Danba, we were accosted by another form of beauty, the vegetation that had turned burning red. We squeezed out our arms from the sardine can the taxi had become to impose our cameras on this show that nature had put up with no one particular in mind. Sitting Bull brought us back to reality, 'International friend, don't get too excited. Keep your head inside the car. There may be policemen on the way. I am only supposed to carry 12 passengers. So if I see the police I will ask you to lie low, okay? And you two ladies too, please.'

At 1,800 m, Danba was at a considerably lower elevation than what we had got accustomed to. As we descended from Bamei through a narrow road surrounded by high cliffs, the autumnal red gave way to different shades of green. It also felt a lot warmer.

The valley of Danba was home to the Qiang people, an ancient tribe distinct from the Tibetans and Hans. While over the course of their long history of living along the Sino-Tibetan frontier, the Qiang had embraced many aspects of both Han and Tibetan culture, many still followed a unique religion. Known in China as the 'White Stone Religion', its followers believed that every object in life was endowed with a soul that was worth worshipping. They also revered white stones, found all over the valley, as symbols of their deities. The Qiang people, therefore, placed white stones along their roof walls and in the centre of houses, crossroads, shrines and any important site.

Thousands of people had already arrived at Danba. The show was on and it was impossible to get a seat or even secure a view. So we just spent time at the fringes soaking up the atmosphere. Hawkers were floating with large hydrogen balloons, dropping a little closer to earth as their sales went up. Women were selling beads to anyone who still had some spare space on her neck. Other items on sale—knock-off bags, shoes and hats—carpeted the grounds surrounding the podium. Empty packets of instant noodles were building up a mountain along the edges. Han policemen formed a fence guarding the entire space and a young officer explained the rules, 'It's organized every year. Every village here nominates a beauty. I would say there are a hundred contestants to begin with. The first round eliminates two-thirds of them. So 30 of them survive to the last round, which will be held the day after tomorrow. That day, the winner will be given the Golden Flower. There will be two Silver Flowers and three will get Pomegranate Flowers.'

'But it's a pity,' our policeman quipped. 'We can't watch any of it. We have to stand guard with our backs facing the beauties.'

We giggled and went inside shamelessly, leaving our forlorn policeman behind.

This time, we managed to get some standing space in the last row. The stands were filled chock-a-block with people of all ages. The females in the audience, in particular, were all dressed as if for their wedding, demanding the attention of the world. They wore black velvety jackets and skirts with heavily embroidered edges. Kilogram-loads of jewellery hung from their necks. The most noticeable aspect, though, was their hair, thick plaited strands running over their foreheads decorated by big silver brooches and flaps of cloth called haze covering the rest of the hair all the way to the nape. Colourful tassels swung from the tip of this cloth.

Some activists had taken issue with the organization of such festivals and the accompanying mass-ethnic dressing that was promoted for these events as being part of the Chinese government's attempts to neatly box minorities into exotic singing-dancing stereotypes enjoying 24/7 happiness. Judging by this heavily dressed turnout at Danba, the audience didn't seem to care much for this argument.

One after another, each contestant came to present a cameo to the judges. Most girls sang songs in Tibetan or Mandarin. Some uttered formal proses glorifying Danba. A few tried dancing to Bollywood tunes. One girl tried a ramp walk, while another even made a pigeon disappear. The highlights of the event were their errors, stutters, falls, stage fright and forgetfulness.

At mid-day, the results for the first round were announced. The judges noted, as in every contest, that this year the quality was 'especially good' and they had a 'tough time' choosing the winners. The group of young students standing next to me murmured that this year's contestants were the worst they had seen.

The compere announced the registration numbers of the ones selected. The list was announced again. After that, there was a big rush for the exit as the failed contestants and their families fled. The chosen few occupied the centre stage. Their families and extended families joined them as did a handful of tourists, mostly old Han men, who were clicking photographs like possessed maniacs. More than the contestants, it was their heavily decorated grandmothers who were getting the most attention. I spoke with one of the shortlisted girls as her grandmother, half of Lhamo's height, grinned beside her. Lhamo, the chosen beauty, was studying mass communications in a university in Chengdu and hoped to work in the tourism sector some day.

'I am so happy,' Lhamo said. 'I had been practising for this for the last six months. The toughest part of the preparations is to know about Danba's history and culture. The judges can ask any question on that. But my family helped me a lot. Whenever I had some query about our culture, I could ask my brothers and cousins. And if they didn't know the answer, there was always my grandmother.'

I asked if she had been nervous on the stage.

'Yes, of course. Even after all the preparations, anything can happen. If something goes wrong, it is so shameful. All the people from my village are here. So are people from all the other villages around here. My family would lose face. My village would lose face. I don't know how my three minutes passed. I have no memory of that time. I am just very happy.'

I asked her about how she would prepare for the finals to be held the day after. Lhamo said, 'I don't know. I just want to have a good meal with my family now.'

The narrow streets of Danba were transformed as they were filled with extravagantly dressed men and women looking for lunch. Since there were only so many cooks in town, the majority, including us, resorted to instant noodles from the supermarkets. Soon all the curbstones in Danba got taller as people sat on them with their steaming bowls.

We were seated next to a man who looked like a great wanderer. His face was so rugged that I could almost spot lichens growing over it. His clothes peeled off, clinging on to his body like a dying vine. He was attracting passers-by who paused to admire the pendant he was wearing, a doughnut-sized ivory ring. They came and touched it, rubbed it, and asked if he wanted to sell it. He wouldn't, and he also wouldn't eat instant noodles, but just sat there and smiled at the world, a smile from a thousand years ago.

Lobo had a sudden brainwave that she too must walk like the Qiang. We visited a tailor's shop, of which there was one too many in Danba, to get her a quick fix. The shop was next to a gambling den which had two fortune tellers sitting outside its doors, making perfect sense.

The tailor's shop was run by a middle-aged Tibetan couple who in their mannerisms appeared to be the manifestations of deities for honesty and simplicity. With hushed voices, gentle smiles and a lot of patience, they let Lobo try on their entire collection till she chose the cheapest ensemble, just a hair makeover to make her face look like the locals. As we were about to leave, two young girls dressed in jeans and T-shirts rushed in. They seemed to be in great hurry.

'Please fix it quickly,' one of the girls said, handing over her skirt. 'The back has slit open. I have nothing else to wear for the finals.'

Danba, besides being the valley of beauties, was also the valley of flies. To keep the insects busy, the town had dug in an enormous collection of plastic flowers into the streets.

As the night set in, howling winds swam into this town sandwiched between steep hills, construction debris and the Dadu River. Hui Muslims, good salespeople as always, began swarming the streets selling peanuts. Makeshift barbecue grills with tables and chairs sprung up at every crossroad.

Hoping for an unforgettable cultural experience, we walked into a building named 'Tibetan Performance Centre', only to find out that it was a KTV. With nothing else to do, we spent hours inside a Tibetan restaurant where the children of the owners watched me closely for the entire duration that we were there, without saying a word. As we were paying the bill, the mother of the two asked me, 'So you are an Indian. But are you Han or are you Tibetan?'

The next day, we woke up early to get Lobo dressed up for the show. She tried her best to mimic the locals but as we were leaving the hotel, the mother of the lady who managed the place yelled, 'Look at her! Come back. Come back.'

We wondered if we had violated any custom.

'Poor girl! You don't have any nice jewellery. And your clothes look cheap. Don't worry. I will give you my clothes and jewellery.'

We protested but the mother and the daughter had suddenly got a life-mission.

'We might as well change your haze. And I will give you a skirt too.'

The mother–daughter duo spent a good one hour dressing up and adorning Lobo. The son-in-law, who then had to look after their young baby, didn't seem too pleased. He kept slamming the door of their bedroom frequently. All throughout, we kept on thanking the family for their kindness.

'You are the guest of our hotel,' the mother smiled. 'We have to make sure you look good.'

Once Lobo was fully made over, they looked

pleased with all the effort. Indeed, if she had a copper tone to her skin, she would have easily passed as a Qiang woman.

'These are clothes and jewellery from my wedding,' the mother said. 'Looking at you, I suddenly feel like it is my wedding day today.'

We joined the horde of traditionally dressed villagers in the stadium. Lobo sat, uninvited, with a group of young women while I found a vantage point near the entrance to the stage from where I could photograph anyone who would make an appearance. Today was the day for performances that were part of the Beauty Festival but not related to the contest. Hundreds of elderly men and women made a beeline for the stage and once on it, arranged themselves in concentric circles. The men wore white wide-brimmed hats, high red boots, layers of animal skin robes, and thick fancy waist and shoulder belts with large metal motifs. The women wore the same dresses from the previous day. The group sang sombre tunes and danced in simple moves, a little wave of the hand, a short jump, moving along as part of a spiral galaxy.

The most exaggerated moves came from the man at the head of this enormous coiling-uncoiling serpent. His jumps were the highest and his hand sways, holding a white scarf, the wildest. Sometimes the group would nominate this man to stand at the centre and then one by one, the dancers would come and place their scarves on his extended hands. A mountain of scarves would form on his hands and then the song would end. The scarfs would then be taken back by everyone who had contributed them. It was all very formal, very decorative and very geriatric.

While I was busy taking photographs, Lobo chatted with one of the ladies sitting next to her. She happened to be a Silver Flower winner from a previous edition of the contest. Her name was Dorje Xiamu (real name). She was 32 years old and had two young children, a son and a daughter.

'I come from a very poor family,' she told Lobo. 'We are farmers. The government supports families like ours with 200 yuan per year.'

Lobo asked her how she had prepared for the contest.

'Every village recommends a person for this,' she noted. 'Usually she is someone who is already reputed as a beauty. In my time, there wasn't much of talent contest like now. It was just about height, figure and appearance. So we could just dress well and show up. My life didn't change much after winning. I just got 500 yuan as a prize. I have only four years of education, which is why I couldn't leverage much from my win. Nowadays, the winners are mostly university students or those working in cities. So once they win they can make a lot more out of their lives.'

'I got married at a very young age,' she said. 'I was only 18. When I see you and get to know more about you, I feel so proud of you. Because, you are able to work in a job despite being a woman and you are working in Singapore. That is so nice.'

Dorje had bolder plans for her future.

'I want to start a homestay soon. We are still very poor. I haven't bought any new clothes for two years, although a tourist from Chongqing gave me some of her old clothes. So if I can start a business, things will be better for us.'

As the event was coming to a close, Lobo said farewell to the ladies and joined me at my vantage point. The crowd and the performers saw the two of us together—a foreigner and a lady dressed as a Danba girl—and drew its own inferences. A queue suddenly formed before us, demanding to get photographed beside us. We obliged happily as plus-sized Tibetan elderly people, all dressed in someone's wedding wear just as Lobo was, hugged us and posed. And there I was, the odd man out, in a sweaty T-shirt and dusty jeans, the giggling nobody getting his fix in a Madame Tussaud's Museum. A local journalist joined in and asked me some banal questions about how I felt about the event.

'It is so nice to have a foreigner here,' she said. 'Your presence has made the event complete.'

As the queue extended, we felt rather ashamed, wondering whether we were stealing the limelight from the honourable guests who had come to attend the event. Noticing the commotion, the Han tourists jumped into the fray. Mobile phones made way for bazooka cameras held by middle-aged Han men wearing sleeveless khaki jackets with enough pockets to fit in any insurance-disclaimer statement. Lobo waved at them vigorously, 'Excuse me,' she pleaded. 'I am a fake. I am not a local.'

The photographers didn't seem to care one bit. Snap, snap and more snaps. Like trapped gazelles, we swerved directions and walked hurriedly for the exit.

In the afternoon, we visited the villages around Danba. Little did we know that this short excursion would turn us into side characters in a love story so well suited for Danba. We found Sitting Bull again at the town's borders.

'Hey international friend!' he said, looking overjoyed. 'We meet again. How are the beauties treating you? You will be jealous to know that they have been treating me very well. My business has been so good ferrying the contestants back and forth.'

We asked him if he could take us around the villages.

'Of course I can. But you know the rule well. You two have to pay me at least 20.'

Lobo protested, 'Can't you see my dress? I am a local person. Give me the local rate.'

Sitting Bull took a close look at Lobo. 'No, lady. The necklace you are wearing is from Sertar. This proves you are not local. So no local rates for you. But wait, I know someone who will surely take you there for cheap.'

He disappeared and came back with a lean man in his 30s.

'This is Dawa. He will take you around. And hope to see you again, international friend.'

Once we had completed our tour, we realized that the man had indeed asked for a very low price.

As soon as we got inside his car, Dawa gave us his card. It featured small cartoonish portraits of Barack Obama, Osama bin Laden and others. Lobo translated the card for me:

*No matter who you are, I can give you a lift.*Obama's speech bubble said, *'If you take the car, we will gift you an American green card.'*

Sola Aoi, an AV idol, that is, said, *'Me, a teacher, also likes to sit in this car.'*

Yao Ming, the basketball star, said, *'Take a ride, just for happiness.'*

Sister Feng, a Chinese internet celebrity, notorious for her bold marriage flier and never-ending supply of bad-taste comments, said, *'If anyone throws away this card, I'll marry him.'* (I still retain the card)

Osama bin Laden said, *'I guarantee that there is a bomb in this car.'*

Dawa came from Daofu, a town nearer to Sertar. He was a talkative man.

'Men from Daofu are the best,' he said. 'They are famously handsome and dress well. Men from Danba are also famous—as drunkards, smokers and as Tibetans with the worst fashion sense. That's why men from Daofu can get many girls outside of their town and girls from Daofu have to become nuns.'

With his unbuttoned shirt over a white vest, Dawa did have a fashion sense rather different from the unwashed layer-upon-another-layer dressing style that we had encountered thus far in our trip.

Our first stop was Jiaju, selected in 2005 by Chinese National Geography magazine as the most beautiful village in China. The villagers, after reading the article on the magazine, began charging for entry into the village. A ticketing point manned with no-nonsense villagers made sure that no crow passed through for free. The village, comprising around a hundred miniature castle-like houses spread along a wide hill, did not really live up to its reputation (this statement should not be seen as a progressive agenda to reduce entry prices for future generations to this village). The houses were freshly painted and looked very similar to the mud castles of the Maghreb region in northwest Africa. Corn cobs were spread neatly on their white rooftops and bright red chillies adorned the brown facades. Homestay signs completed the decoration. Jiaju appeared to be the most prosperous village we had visited thus far in our trip. A magazine article had turned it into a commercialized fairyland without an American brand.

Dawa dropped us at a vantage point.

'You two walk around,' he said. 'In the meantime, I will brush my teeth and take a shower.'

We saw him heading towards a mountain spring. We walked around and got bored soon. But we decided to give Dawa enough time for a shower. We walked over to a platform overlooking the entire valley. Friendly locals followed us to sell juicy pears from the mountains. Friendly Han tourists followed too, again mistaking Lobo for a local. Lobo tried her best again, 'I am a fake! I am a fake!'

One middle-aged man in cameraman jackets said, 'It's okay, as long as the spirit of this place is there.'

One middle-aged lady who was snapping us busily with her mobile phone said, 'No one would know back in Wuhan where you are from.'

We asked the paparazzi to guess what country I came from. The responses came thick and fast—Nigeria, Africa, Tanzania, Argentina, Pakistan, Afghanistan.

When we went back to where Dawa had dropped us, he was changing into a fresh set of clothes. 'Sorry, sorry,' he said. 'I haven't had a shower for days. Since the stream was near, I thought why not clean up a bit.'

He took us next for a quick look from far at Suopo, the village with the most well-preserved towers that Danba was famous for. These towers, made of solid stone, were scattered all around the Danba valley. The village of Suopo itself had around 80 towers. Some of the towers were up to 1,800 years old. Their primary purpose had been forgotten, but much of what we know about them today is because of the passionate work of Frédérique Darragon, an amateur archaeologist.

The towers came with square or star-shaped bases and were perhaps built to look out for ruffians from neighbouring villages, or perhaps merely for architectural posturing. Many of them just ended up as storerooms. The tallest towers could be as high as 50 metre. These chimney-like towers gave a strange industrial feel to this ancient land and also bore a peculiar resemblance to the ones in the Svaneti region in Georgia and parts of Chechnya.

After we winked at Suopo, Dawa took us to our final stop, the village of Zhonglu. It was a steep climb and the narrow road was in terrible shape. Sensibly, the villagers didn't bother charging any entry fees. The experience of the harrowing drive was sufficient compensation for entering their domain. To add to our misery, Dawa began talking on the phone. At one potent death-bend, he suddenly thrust his mobile phone at Lobo, 'My friend,' he said. 'I told her I have foreigners with me today. Please say something.'

Lobo, already traumatized, was lost for words after saying, 'Hello.'

Dawa took back the phone after the noticeable silence and unleashed his motor-mouth again. Lobo whispered to me in English, 'It's a young woman. I don't think it was his wife.'

Once we got used to the road's twirls and Dawa's antics, Zhonglu appeared pretty. The narrow road was overwhelmed with thick vegetation that varied in colour and density—bright orange leaves came and left, getting replaced by the small flatness of bright green vegetables, then a patch of woodlands, and then autumnal leaves again. Old men in tattered clothes and bent backs carried around heavy loads of firewood. Compared to Jiaju, Zhonglu was a lot more impoverished and a lot less commercialized— authentic, as we tourists loved to call such less fortunate places.

Along the ascending mud track, we drove past a group of young women. Moments later, Dawa stopped the car suddenly.

'My friend will join us,' he said. 'The lady you talked to earlier.'

One of the women we had just passed by caught up with our car. She had left her friends behind. Dawa opened the door for her and she sat down next to Lobo at the back of the car. She was wearing simple clothes unlike the fancy crowd in Danba. She was probably in her mid-30s and had a square jaw and broad nose. Together with her headscarf, she looked very similar to Himachali women from India.

When we started again, Dawa became even more talkative, sometimes in Mandarin, sometimes in Tibetan. The woman looked disinterested and responded in monosyllables. Lobo admired her looks and asked if she could take a photograph of her.

'Later, later,' she said.

Dawa stopped his car again.

'The road ends soon,' he said. 'You two walk the way

up and then you will come across a beautiful point. In the meantime, we will finish some work. We have to deliver noodles to someone here. We will be back before you come. We will just wait for you here.'

Brushing and taking a shower, delivering noodles; Dawa had rather strange chores to do at high altitudes.

As we walked away from the car, Lobo and I whispered our suspicions to each other: 'he said she's a friend, but why meet so secretly, and what are they doing now? Do they really need to deliver noodles?' But the sunlight had begun its parting show on Zhonglu and the Qiang towers, the autumn foliage, and the small green farmlands all worked in sync to create magic. Without realizing it, we forgot the investigative case that we had just begun working on. We waited for sunset at a vantage point, accompanied by a few Han tourists and their tripods. A Tibetan woman had climbed up to set up a makeshift stall for drinks and instant noodles. She had also brought along her cow, which ignored the allure of the sunset to munch on highland vegetation.

It was almost dark when we went back to our car. From outside we saw the silhouette of two heads resting on each other. I knocked on the car window, making the people inside jump. Dawa and the lady came out of the car instantly. Dawa grabbed a bowl of noodles from the dashboard and began eating it in a great rush. His hair was dishevelled and the lady was dusting off mud and straw from her dress. Dawa abandoned the noodles halfway and started his car.

'Not nice,' he said. 'We couldn't deliver it so I was eating it. But it has become cold.'

As we climbed down, the lady became a lot friendlier towards Dawa. She was massaging his neck as he drove and when he went fast at a scary bend, she would say in Mandarin, 'Stupid baby, you are one stupid baby.'

In the dark, driving seemed especially dangerous and at times I could see that nearly half of our tyres were almost over the precipice. But Dawa and the lady were in another world. He extended one hand backwards and the lady grabbed it and began playing with it.

Dawa dropped her at the same spot where we had picked her up earlier. As she departed, she reached out across the seat to give him two long kisses, solving the mystery for us. Dawa confessed right after she left, as if he was in the pulpit and Lobo and I were the priests, 'Isn't she nice?' He didn't wait for our response, continuing, 'She is 38, I am 37. Here, it is very common for people to have multiple affairs because most marriages here are arranged. I have three lovers now, but this one loves me the most. She washes my clothes when my wife is away. I met her along one of my journeys. It's easy for drivers to have affairs here as we pick up girls and drop them so we know their address and we also have their numbers because they call us to book their rides.'

I asked him how he manages the complications that might arise.

'I don't know. Her husband doesn't know about us. No one knows.'

'Her husband is not good. He doesn't take care of her. But I asked her not to divorce him because they have kids. I have two kids also. So I don't want to divorce my wife. Besides, I like my wife. I married her after a lot of hassle. I used to date a Silver Flower winner once but she was only after money. My wife is good. We had met at Kangding University as students. She had a lot of suitors, and many men came to ask for her hand. The custom here is that suitors spend one night at the girl's house and then she is supposed to choose from among them. But my wife rejected everyone and later chose me. My mother didn't like her because people in Daofu say that Danba girls are of mixed blood and so they are not good people. We had to run away to Chengdu for three years. We lived with my wife's sister who was a Golden Flower winner. She was a famed beauty and was staying with a 62-year-old man in Chengdu. She didn't want anyone to know that she was living that way. But the man was rich and they gave us shelter. So we have gone through a lot. I don't want to waste it. I will just meet the other girl on the way like this every day. We will see what fate has in store for us.'

So we survived this torturous road in the valley of beauties where a love story was being enacted out every day. I scorned Dawa, aided by my convenient morality, but I couldn't help pitying him. With his boyish charm, his escapades, his doubts and his simple heart, he was all too human, his life entangled in the valley of beauties between Golden Flowers and

Silver Flowers, far from the legend of the boisterous all-conquering Khampa man. As we said goodbye, Dawa said, 'But remember to pray for me please. I don't dare to pray before Buddha myself because he knows I am a liar. But tell him that he is the one responsible for making my life complicated.'

Epilogue

We left Danba the next morning. Dorje sent us live updates about the finals of the Beauty Contest over WeChat. The road from Danba to Chengdu passed under the shadows of the Siguniang Mountains (Four Sister Mountains). I craned my neck at every bend to catch one more glimpse of the splendid snow-covered peaks, and to look down was to realize how close we were to be set up for a sky burial. And once we descended to Wolong, which was Giant Panda territory, we encountered the worst road in our entire journey. As we were being cradled by this demonic caregiver, a rather apt denouement to our trip, I recollected the images from the days that had just gone by: exhilarating nature, blinding white peaks and their reflections at Yading, the gallery of powdered snow hills in Litang, Mount Yala rising out of nowhere from the Tagong grasslands, and the burning autumn foliage of Bamei. In these remote and sparsely populated highlands, we had encountered a bewildering array of characters: the Khampa men with their anachronistic masculinity, the Khampa women with their perpetual suffering, the charismatic drivers, the nomad families with their cyclical lives, the risk-it-all young entrepreneurs of Daocheng, the revivalist Han monks in Larung, the Catholic church guard in Kangding for whom the Vatican was just a short bus ride away, the beauties of Danba, and the eerie bone-collector in Litang's sky burial site who sang ominously, predicting death. I was even rubbing money on my clothes before paying anyone, just like many Tibetans do to retain their good fortune.

I had hoped that the emphasis of this trip would be on 'Shangri-La'. But it was the 'other' that was often the most conspicuous, the 'other' types of caterpillar fungus, the 'other' capitals of the queendom, the 'other' Panchen Lama, the 'other' Karmapa Lama, the 'other' government in exile, the 'other' versions of history, the 'other' interpretations of every development in the region, the 'other' race, the 'other' Shangri-La.

When our flight took off from Chengdu, I struggled to see the snowy peaks of Kham just one last time. The city's pollution had blanketed everything. Would I ever come back to Tagong, Litang or Sertar? In 30 years, I silently promised Kham. I tried to imagine how it might look then. Would the mountains of Yading harbour giant industrial complexes of water-bottling plants? Would Shangri-La become indistinguishable from Disneyland? Would Han cultural hegemony obliterate every other peculiarity once a mesh of high-speed trains, all-weather roads, and Weibo (microblogging website) accounts spread out in the region? Or would an environment of mutual trust, understanding and accommodation establish itself, if the popularity of Tibetan Buddhism, the Tibetan script and Tibetan music in China becomes more than a passing fad? Who would provide the inspiration, Zhao the Butcher or Ren Naiqiang? Would the idea of the 'other' remain?

Notes

1. *Xinhua*, 'Tibetans leave home to seek new opportunities', *China Tibet Online*, 15 March 2012, http://chinatibet.people. com.cn/96069/7758682.html. (Accessed on 12 March 2016).

2. The 'liuliu' often repeated in the song are meaningless syllables.

3. Melvyn C. Goldstein and Gelek Rimpoche, *A History of Modern Tibet, 1913-1951: The Demise of the Lamaist State* (Berkeley: University of California Press, 1989), p. 46.

4. Peter M. Foggin et al, 'Assessment of the health status and risk factors of Kham Tibetan pastoralists in the alpine grasslands of the Tibetan plateau', *Social Science & Medicine, Elsevier*, vol. 63, issue no. 9 (November 2006): pp. 2512–32.

5. 'Life expectancy in Tibet nearly doubled over last six decades: White paper,' *Xinhua News*, 11 July 2011, https://web. archive.org/web/20131115122122/http://news.xinhuanet.com/english2010/china/2011-07/11/c_13978305.htm. (Accessed on 12 March 2016).

6. Malcolm Moore, '£1 million for world's most expensive dog', *The Telegraph*, 15 March 2011, http://www.telegraph.co.uk/news/worldnews/asia/china/8383084/1-million-for-worlds-most-expensive-dog.html. (Accessed on 23 August 2016).

7. 'Tibet anniversary used to insult Dalai Lama', *Bankok Post*, 9 September 2015, http://www.pressreader.com/thailand/bangkok-post/20150909/281616714143213/TextView; *PTI*, 'Dalai Lama bent on killing innocent Han Chinese: China',

Daily News and Analysis (DNA), 1 September 2011, http://
www.dnaindia.com/world/report-dalai-lama-bent-on-killing-
innocent-han-chinese-china-1582288. (Accessed on 11 April
2016).

8. K. Dhondup, *Songs of the Sixth Dalai Lama* (Dharamsala:
Library of Tibetan Works and Archives, 1981).

9. Ibid.

10. Stephen Kurczy, '"Oriental Yeti" found in China is no
Yeti', *The Christian Science Monitor,* 6 April 2010, http://www.
csmonitor.com/World/Global-News/2010/0406/Oriental-Yeti-
found-in-China-is-no-Yeti. (Accessed on 27 August 2016).

11. Tsering Woeser, Wang Lixiong, Violet S. Law (Editor,
Translator), *Voices From Tibet: Selected Essays and Reportage*
(Honolulu: University of Hawai'i Press, 2014).

12. Karma Phuntso, 'H.H. Khenpo Jigme Phuntsho: A Tribute
and a Translation', *Journal of Bhutan Studies,* 2004.

13. Li Jin, 'Buried Past and Excavated Hope: Larung and
Buddhist interactions between Tibet and China today', 2010.

14. *AFP,* 'Tibetan Buddhist nuns take up feminism and seek
equal status with monks', *South China Morning Post,* 15 March
2016, http://www.scmp.com/lifestyle/article/1924630/tibetan-
buddhist-nuns-take-feminism-and-seek-equal-status-monks.
(Accessed on 5 June 2016).

15. W.Y. Evans-Wentz, *The Tibetan Book of the Dead* (Delhi:
Winsome Books, 2010).

16. Gyanpian Gyamco and Wu Wei, *King Gesar* (Beijing: China
Intercontinental Press; Shenyang: Liaoning Education Press,
2009).

17.   http://www.chinatravel.com/ganzi-attraction/danba-
beauty-valley/ (Accessed on 21 June 2016).

18. Jinba Tenzin, *In the Land of the Eastern Queendom: The
Politics of Gender and Ethnicity on the Sino-Tibetan Border*
(Seattle: University of Washington Press, 2013).